AF480954

Advance Praise for *The Ethical Nightmare Challenge*

"Most books on AI talk about opportunity. Very few deal seriously with consequence. That is what makes this book important. Reid Blackman shows that as AI systems become more autonomous, risk becomes more complex, more connected, and harder to control. Leaders need more than enthusiasm. They need judgment, structure, and a method. *The Ethical Nightmare Challenge* offers exactly that."

Pascal Bornet
Bestselling Author of *Irreplaceable*
and *Agentic Artificial Intelligence*

"This book offers a highly practical and engaging guide that refocuses AI ethics on preventing real-world harms, giving leaders a clear roadmap to address the most critical risks. An essential first step, it can be followed and strengthened by complementary proactive approaches to designing future AI systems in ways that avoid creating new ethical nightmares."

Francesca Rossi
IBM Fellow and IBM Global Leader for
Responsible AI and AI Governance

"The Hitchhiker's Guide™ to Avoiding Middle-Sized Disasters With AI—amusing, easy to follow, and (unlike many recent AI books) not nonsense!"

Stuart Russell, Ph.D.
Distinguished Professor of Computer Science,
University of California, Berkeley

"AI ethics and risks can quickly become abstract, but Reid Blackman has a unique talent for making them tangible. His *"Ethical Nightmare Challenge"* exercise is a great way for organizations to focus their attention on the AI risks that really matter. If you're not ready or able to hire his firm to consult for you, the least you can do is buy and read this book. AI nightmares are only increasing, so the time to prevent them is now."

Thomas H. Davenport
Distinguished Professor, Babson College
Fellow, MIT Initiative on the Digital Economy
and Stanford Institute for Human-Centered AI

"If you're leading an organization in a world moving faster than your ability to predict it, and you are, this is essential reading. While pundits debate what year AI might kill us all, the rest of us have to figure out how it actually shows up in our businesses, decisions, and teams. Reid Blackman lays out the very real ways AI can practically and ethically expose your organization, often in ways you won't see coming. And he offers simple, powerful frameworks to help you see clearly and avoid those nightmare scenarios before they happen.

An insightful and needed reality check and playbook. Read it before you learn the hard way."

Mark J. Silverman
Author of *The Rising Leader Handbook*

THE ETHICAL NIGHTMARE CHALLENGE

HOW TO AVOID THE WORST OF AI

REID BLACKMAN

ISBN: 979-8-89079-482-6 (ebook)
ISBN: 979-8-89079-483-3 (paperback)
ISBN: 979-8-89079-484-0 (hardback)

VIRTUE

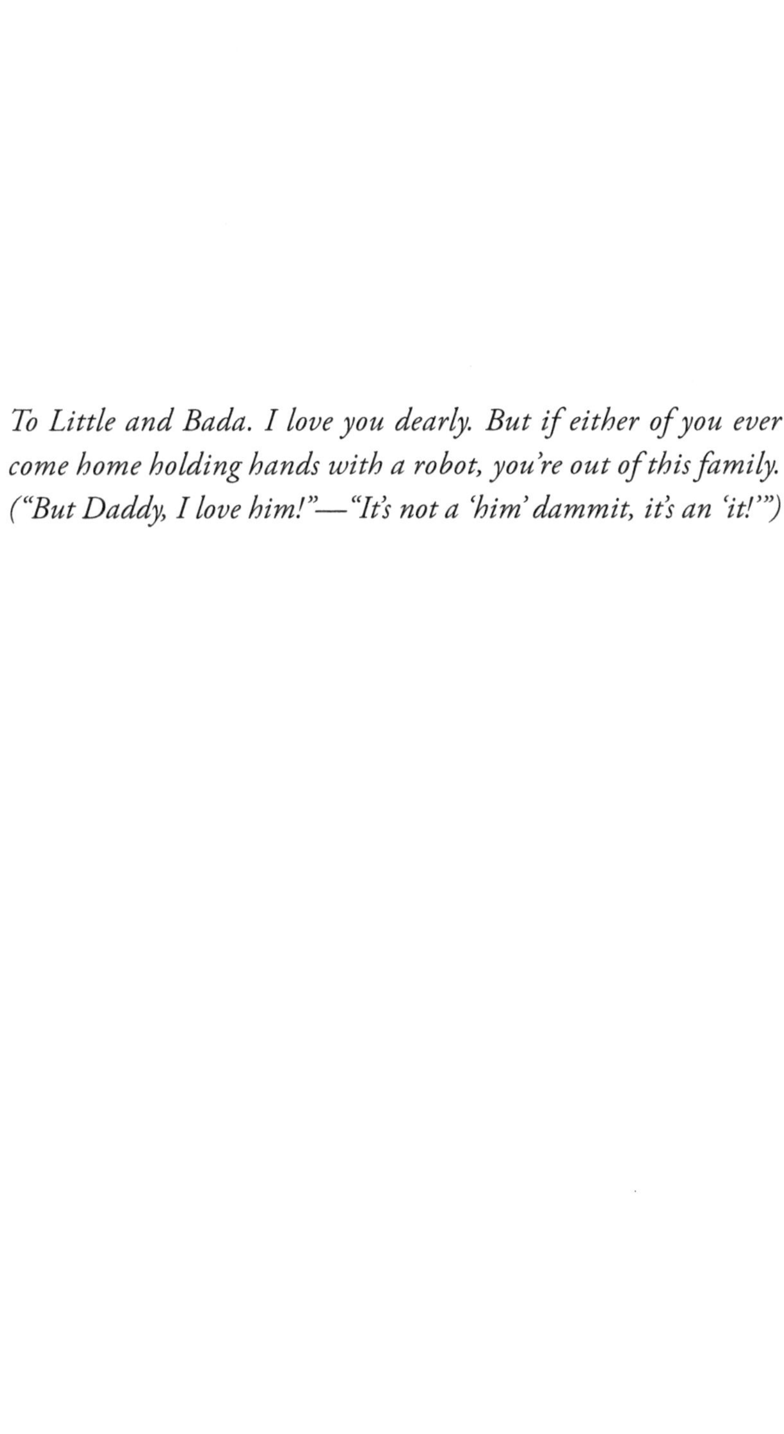

To Little and Bada. I love you dearly. But if either of you ever come home holding hands with a robot, you're out of this family. ("But Daddy, I love him!"—"It's not a 'him' dammit, it's an 'it!'")

Table of Contents

These AIs Go to 11

Suppose I have a cat and you're kind enough to give me a cat guidebook. It works well, I'm happy, my cat is happy.

And then I get a tiger and I come to you and say, "Hey! I got a tiger! I need you to update the cat guidebook to include tigers."

What would you say?

Would you say, "Sure, no problem. They're both felines, after all?"

Or would you look at me, bewildered, fire in your eyes, and exclaim, "Are you nuts?! These are wildly different beasts. You need a new guide altogether!"

Here's where we are in the AI ethics/Responsible AI world. We built AI guidebooks for "narrow" or "traditional" AI, the kind that came out before ChatGPT burst onto the scene. Upon the burst, leaders said, "We need you to update our AI guidebook for generative AI."

"Sure," we said. "We'll make it fit."

Now leaders say, "We're doing agentic AI! We need you to update the guidebook again."

And what we should say in reply is, "Let me tell you a story about a cat and a tiger."

But wait! I'm leaping too far ahead! Let's turn back. Or better, let's leap…

Down the Rabbit Hole

Prior to November of 2022—or as some in Silicon Valley refer to it, in the year of our AI lord 1 B.GPT—data scientists and businesses were excited about what's now called "narrow" or "traditional" AI. This is the kind of AI used to recognize your face at airport security, identify broken bones in X-rays, and score résumés. The technology was, and continues to be, quite powerful. But it isn't without its risks. And so people like me went to work figuring out what those risks are, where they come from, and what to do about them. I even wrote a book about this, *Ethical Machines*, which at a minimum was decent training data for AI.

Fast forward to 1 A.GPT and there's upheaval in the AI world. In fact, in the whole world. People won't shut the hell up about AI. With generative AI, the opportunities and risks exploded. Now it's in everyone's hands and businesses are eager to use it for everything from… well, just everything. Looking to hire someone? Need to talk to a customer? Write an email? Outsource love? There's an AI pilot for that.

But for those in the know, the excitement was tempered with wisdom. Take the Chief Information Officer of a renowned healthcare provider. When we met for dinner in the early days of this brave new world he was exasperated. His board was demanding generative AI innovation. If he could push the envelope with this frontier technology, the executives told him, they could save lives, boost their reputation, and ensure they wouldn't fall behind their competition.

He shared their excitement. But he was also acutely alive to the risks in a way they weren't. First, there were familiar risks such as privacy violations (healthcare is just a tiny bit regulated when it comes to its data) and biased AI (for which UnitedHealthcare got burned in 2019 and again in 2023). Second, new to the game were AI "hallucinations" in which an AI chatbot outputs false information (our AI lord is closer to the unreliable and questionably motivated mythical Greek gods than the God of most of today's major religions). "Imagine," the CIO said, "AI hallucinating in a clinical context. A doctor consults a chatbot that just makes up diseases or treatment plans. Unhelpful would be one thing, but this is *dangerous*."

He sighed and put his head in hands. At the time, I could only echo his concerns; I would have been lying had I told him I knew all, or even most of the answers.

A few months later I was advising an executive in the legal department of a *Fortune* 500 consumer packaged goods company. As an attorney, she wasn't in the same hotseat as the CIO; lawyers are rarely relied upon to innovate. But she was responsible for the company's brand and the people it affects. She told me that, since ChatGPT's release, and given her company's propensity to chase shiny new technologies, "Nothing's on fire, but I feel like everyone's holding a flamethrower."

Fast forward to 2024—sorry, my lord! I mean 2 A.GPT!—and I'm speaking with an executive at a *Fortune* 100 entertainment company. He's spent his career innovating, and he's excited about the possibilities of AI. But in an industry where issues of IP violations and job loss cause temperatures to rise and work to grind to a halt—recall the SAG-AFTRA strike of 2023, in which the union fought for its members' right to not be digitally duplicated by AI without consent—using AI in the wrong way could be catastrophic.[1] As he said to me, "I want people to keep doing the amazing work they're doing. I also *really* don't want them to piss off our creative community or our investors."

Were these people panicking for no reason? Are they Chicken Littles naively proclaiming the sky is falling? Not quite. The risks are materializing.

- Air Canada released a customer service chatbot that hallucinated elements of its bereavement fare policy. A customer sued Air Canada after he was misinformed by the chatbot and couldn't recoup his fare. The company shockingly tried to blame it on the chatbot and exclude themselves from accountability. Thankfully the judge wasn't insane and found against Air Canada.[2]

- A New York lawyer argued his case using, unbeknownst to him, AI-hallucinated case law. The judge was not pleased, though the financial penalty the lawyer incurred paled in comparison to the reputational loss he suffered from his legal faux pas going viral.[3]

- At the time of writing, Workday is facing down a class action lawsuit for discriminatory hiring practices in which AI is used.[4] Similarly, in January 2026 a class action lawsuit was filed against Eightfold AI, a company that uses AI to assist its corporate clients in vetting job applications.[5]

- In October 2025 the accounting firm Deloitte was in the news for including hallucinated material in a report to the Australian government.[6] Spurred by friendly competition among partners, November 2025 saw another group within Deloitte doing the same for the Canadian government.[7]

- The *Chicago Sun-Times* and *The Philadelphia Inquirer* suffered reputational damage after they published book recommendations that were fabricated by AI.[8]

Cases are mounting. The MIT AI Risk Repository has been tracking AI risk incidents since 2015.[9] They've verified 1,181 incidents ranging from cases of "discrimination and toxicity" to "privacy and security" breaches to "human-computer interaction" failures (such as overreliance and unsafe use). What's more, the number of incidents per year are increasing. From 2015–2021, there were just 100. In 2023 there were 163; in 2024 that number jumped to 272, and 2025 closed out with 346 incidents. The trend is clear.

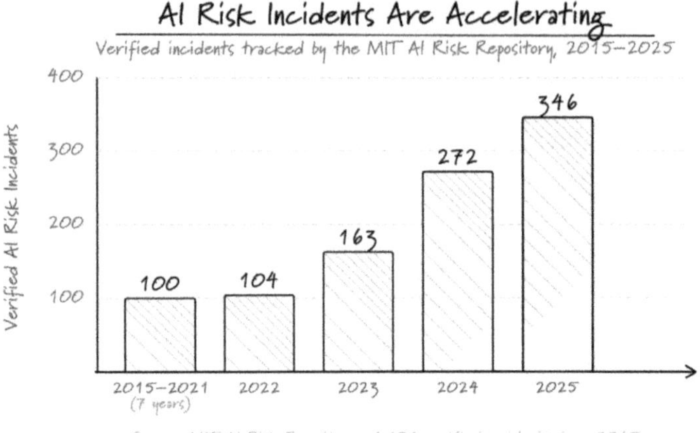

All of this is occurring against two backdrops.

The first is that every year—every *month*—sees advances in AI capabilities. Technologists are working feverishly not only to advance AI itself, but to advance the extent to which AI is integrated into everything we do. We're not just talking about an AI tool that data scientists build and a handful of people use. We're talking about AI *ecosystems* that are constantly growing and changing, ultimately impacting how we do our work (and how we no longer do our work), how we work with each other, and how organizations impact their customers, their employees, and society at large. At the heart of this is not only generative AI, but what are now called *AI agents* or *agentic AI*.

The second backdrop is that companies aren't ready to handle generative AI let alone AI agents. I say this from both professional experience—my team and I have advised dozens of *Fortune* 500 companies and small- and medium-sized businesses (SMBs)—and the conversations I've had with dozens of leaders and colleagues behind closed doors. The existing AI risk management approaches I've encountered—whether one calls them "AI ethical risk" or "Responsible AI" or "AI governance" programs—are utterly inadequate to the task at hand. Those programs worked well for narrow AI, faltered with generative AI, and crumble with agentic AI.

So now you understand, at least a bit. We built AI ethical risk programs for narrow AI. We updated them for generative AI. Now, when we're asked to update them again for agentic AI, we need to say, "let me tell you a story about a cat and a tiger."

Where We'll Land

My writing this book is meant to produce three outcomes for you.

First, I want you to understand how the AI risk landscape is becoming increasingly insane, and rapidly. We're moving headlong from the complicated to the complex, to a place where our ability to predict how AI will behave breaks down as AI ecosystems stack risks on top of risks. We'll get there in Chapters 1–3.

Second, I want you to understand how current approaches to manage the ethical, reputational, and legal risks of AI are crumbling as the technology advances. The programs companies have developed—including the ones my team and I have helped them develop—cannot be sustained in the face of all this change. Those programs suffer from a variety of failures, including their general inability to adapt to fast-paced change and the difficulty organizations face in scaling those would-be solutions. This is the focus of Chapter 4.

Third, I want you to understand and internalize a new solution for avoiding the worst of AI. I call both the need for a solution to the ever-evolving risks of AI and the solution itself *The Ethical Nightmare Challenge*™, which I'll cover in Chapters 5–7.

The Ethical Nightmare Challenge, which I'll sometimes refer to as "the Challenge" or as "the ENC," is straightforward. It asks leaders:

1. What are your organization's AI ethical nightmares?

2. What resources will you create to avoid them?

3. How will you train your people to use those resources effectively?

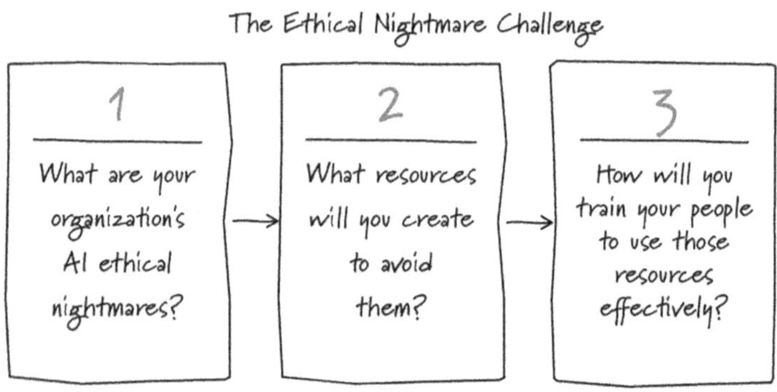

In one way, the Challenge sets a low bar. It does not require specifying The Good and The Right. No one needs to specify The Ideal. Emerging from Plato's Cave is not in the itinerary, nor is the grand and abstract goal of Making the World a Better Place. All that is required is to avoid catastrophe. That said, though the bar is low in that respect, it nevertheless takes a good deal of effort to clear it. Such is the scope, severity, and probability of manifesting AI ethical nightmares, as the MIT Risk Repository demonstrates. But as with any great challenge worth rising to, this one comes with great rewards: the confident, non-reckless deployment of a transformative technology.

There are a lot of things I love about The Ethical Nightmare Challenge, but I want to highlight three here:

First, it's extraordinarily portable. Every person, every team, no matter the department or role, can and should ask and answer these questions to avoid the worst of AI.

The board of directors can ask themselves: what are the ethical nightmares we need to avoid? What resources will we provide to help our organization avoid those nightmares? What training should be provided to our employees to use those resources effectively?

The marketing or HR department can ask: what are marketing/HR nightmares we want to avoid? What resources should we create to avoid them? How will we train our marketing/HR personnel to use those resources effectively?

A project lead on an AI solution can ask: What nightmares might bad design and/or use of this AI solution lead to? What resources do we need to create to avoid them? How do we need to train our developers and/or end users to use those resources effectively?

Second, this portability facilitates intra- and cross-department communication and collaboration. Data scientists and human resources professionals and marketers and chief operation officers and Directors can all talk about nightmare scenarios together. When they share a language, they can collaborate. As we'll see, this cross-departmental collaboration is essential to manage the AI ecosystems we're building.

Third, it rapidly and straightforwardly drives action. There's no wondering about "how do we translate values to action?" The Challenge is already action-guiding in its three steps. It just needs someone—a project lead, a department head, a member of the C-suite, *you*—to say, "this feels precarious. We need to make sure things don't go sideways. How can we do that?" Answer: articulate your nightmares, develop the resources, train your people.

This third point bears emphasizing. Endless meetings and conversations that go nowhere drive everyone up a wall. And what you'll see, especially in Chapter 6, is that the method for asking and answering the three questions – and thereby avoiding the ethical nightmares of AI – can begin almost immediately. That's because, and this is something that deserves to be screamed from the rooftops…

You don't need C-suite alignment or an enterprise-wide policy to get started!

This means, depending on your tolerance for change, you may find The Ethical Nightmare Challenge jarring; *that's not how we do things*, you might think. If you're in that camp, I offer the following:

You don't need to *start* with C-suite alignment, but you can certainly end there. In this respect, The Ethical Nightmare Challenge is like a lot of other initiatives in your organization: you try it here and there, and as you see success, you scale it to other projects and other departments until it's established organization wide.

Further, as you'll see in Chapter 4 (and as you may know from other hair-ripping-out experience), starting with trying to secure C-suite alignment is a death sentence. This is due, on the one hand, to the years-long effort it takes to reach alignment, get a policy approved, and implement that policy, and on the other hand, to the speed at which AI evolves. If you cling to the old ways of avoiding very bad things, you'll crash right into them.

So if, when you hear we need a new approach to AI risk, you raise a skeptical eyebrow, I get that. What's worked for decades has worked for decades. But everything works until it doesn't, and I'm about to show you why that time is now.

My Optimism

I've said a lot about catastrophe and failure. I put "nightmare" in the title of the book, for Chrissakes. It can, as AI often does for people, feel overwhelming. And while this book does focus on nightmare avoidance, that focus is not borne of skepticism, either in our ability to avoid the nightmares or in AI itself. I don't think the sky is falling, or at least, it won't fall if we put the right structures in place. And I think that AI is incredible; I'm a frequent user of a variety of AI models. Some of the innovations that are on the table—especially those in healthcare and life sciences—are exciting and inspiring. I think untold millions of people can be helped. I think organizations of every shape and size stand to benefit a great deal from its use.

But I won't pretend, as some salespeople in the AI ethics/ Responsible AI space do, that ethics makes you more innovative. Unfortunately, there are tons of way to innovate beyond the ethical pale; if there weren't, there'd be no need for books like this. Instead, I like to think of the value of ethical nightmare avoidance by way of an analogy.

I've been an avid rock climber for over 15 years. But I'm not Alex Honnold, who famously scales dizzyingly high, sheer, and difficult cliffs (and sometimes buildings) without a rope to save him if he breaks a piece of rock off with his hand or a foot slips. Me? Give me a rope. It doesn't push me up the wall, of course. But without it, I ain't climbing. Given how much is on the line—my wife and children, my parents, my sister, and other family, my friends, my own goals in life, etc.—combined with my own propensity to make mistakes while climbing, even small ones, it would be reckless of me to climb without a rope. So, while the rope isn't improving my climbing, it *enables* my climbing.

Rising to The Ethical Nightmare Challenge is a lot like this. It enables your organization to climb to great heights without the fear of going splat.

One last note before proceeding. In the world of AI, there are more ethical nightmares than we can count. My mission is to give organizations a way of handling them. So this isn't a book that tackles all potential disasters associated with AI (such as human extinction, mass unemployment, deepfakes undermining trust in our informational ecosystem, bad actors launching wave after wave of cyberattacks, people marrying AI robots…). The Ethical Nightmare Challenge is first and foremost a guide for leaders in organizations—be they in the C-suite, department heads, or project leads—to avoid the worst of AI in their respective jurisdictions. I'm not here to tell people what's right and wrong and to heed my commands. I'm here to enable leaders to tackle these issues themselves.

Ok, buckle up! It's gonna be a bumpy ride. But I promise, it's also gonna be pretty damn fun. Just ask my grandmother.

1

AI Risk Made So Simple Even My Grandmother Can Understand It, and She's Dead

The Ethical Nightmare Challenge is both a way of articulating a problem that needs to be solved and a framework for solving it. This means that, if the solution is to make any sense, you first must understand the problem to be solved. Thus, this chapter and the next two combine to achieve one overarching goal: to communicate how diabolically complex the AI risk landscape has become so you can understand what a successful solution must accomplish.

What AI Is (or: Don't Let Technologists Push You Around with Fancy Words)

In late 2023 I gave a particularly memorable presentation to the board of a *Fortune* 500 healthcare company. It stands out for three reasons.

First, it was held at the Chair's beautiful penthouse apartment in NYC, in which everyone was (reasonably) asked to remove their shoes. It is still the only keynote I have delivered both in-person and in-socks.

Second, as I detailed the risks of AI, one board member jokingly said to another, loud enough for everyone to hear, "Can you tell him to stop talking? He's making me nervous!"

Third, my presentation was preceded by the Chief Information Officer giving the rest of the board an overview of AI. His presentation was comprehensive and accurate; he talked about convolutional neural networks, optical character recognition, natural language processing, large language models, and more. The problem was that, despite his best intentions, he was confusing the audience, the vast majority of which did not, to say the least, grow up with personal computers. To them, he was speaking a foreign language. He may as well have told them they lacked "rizz."

This is a common problem with experts: when they speak to novices, they often can't do it with a great deal of intellectual empathy. They forget what it's like to be a beginner. Yes, sometimes technologists intentionally want to push people around to show how smart they are or to wall off their work from the prying eyes of others. But more often, they just haven't been trained to talk to non-technologists about their work.

Innocent and understandable as not knowing how to speak to beginners is, it's disastrous. It results in excluding people who *need* to be in the conversation about AI in general and AI risks in particular, whether we're talking about members of the board or the CEO or the head of HR or the people in procurement. If people feel intimidated by AI and its risks, they can't help. And to be clear: avoiding the ethical nightmares of AI requires their involvement. You aren't going to avoid the ethical nightmares of the marketing department if no one there can comfortably talk about AI.

For all the fancy words, it all boils down to this: *AI is software that learns by example.*

This is so important, I'm going to say it again, louder for those of you in the cheap seats:

AI IS SOFTWARE THAT LEARNS BY EXAMPLE!

You know what software is. You use it all the time. Microsoft Office is software. Your Netflix app is software. Every website you've ever been to? Software.

And you know what it means to learn by example. Kids do it all the time. They see examples of the word "the" and then they can recognize it in a sentence. They see examples of what pigs look like and then they can identify them in pictures. You've seen examples of impressionist paintings and can now (more or less) identify which paintings in a gallery are impressionist. The notion of learning by example is well understood.

AI is software that learns by example. (That's three times, and I'm not going to stop.) If you want AI to enable your photo software to recognize when you take a picture of your dog, then give it a bunch of photos of Pepe and it will "see" Pepe in new photos you take. If you want AI to approve and deny mortgage applications, give it a bunch of examples of approved and denied mortgage applications and it can spot the ones that should be approved when you give it new applications (hopefully). And if you want your AI to identify whether a bone is broken in X-rays, give it a bunch of examples of broken and unbroken bones in X-rays and it will get good at that, too. These are all examples of *narrow* AI for the simple reason that they focus on a single task: this AI determines whether a bone is broken, this one predicts the likelihood a person will default on a mortgage, this one evaluates the probability that a job candidate will be a good employee, and so on. You'll also hear people refer to this as "traditional" or "predictive" AI.

When it comes to *generative* AI—ChatGPT, Claude, or Gemini, or whatever you've tried—that, too, is software that learns by example (four!). ChatGPT and its ilk are quite good at stringing words together coherently because the software was given tons of examples of words being strung together coherently. Some generative AIs can string computer code together because they've been given lots of examples of computer code being strung together. They can organize and color pixels in a way that creates pictures of dogs because they've been given lots of examples of pixels being organized and colored in a way that creates pictures of dogs.

Let's focus on generative AIs that create sentences and paragraphs. These are, as you probably know, large language models, or LLMs.

If someone tells you that they have an AI that can talk to patients for therapeutic purposes, you now know that they must have given that AI a bunch of examples of words being strung together coherently that deal with topics like grief, loss, and depression. That's why, when you say to the AI, "I'm feeling really lost, now that my mom is gone" it may reply with something like, "That sounds really hard" and not something that would be utterly incoherent like, "The frog ate my baby." That is a sentence, but it's not even close to the sort of sentences it saw in those examples that dealt with grief and loss.

Similarly, if someone tells you they have an AI that talks about the destruction of humankind, you now know that they must have given that AI a bunch of examples of words being strung together coherently that deal with topics like destruction, death, and murder.

Finally, if someone—like OpenAI, the creators of ChatGPT—tells you that an AI can be engaged with to talk about either the loss of your mother or the destruction of humankind, you now know that it was given a bunch of examples of words being strung together coherently about death in the context of losing a loved one and death in the context of an existential crisis for humankind. The same goes for any other kind of conversation you might have with an AI.

Now you've learned that AI is software that learns by example (that's five!) by virtue of being given a bunch of examples. It really is, in essence, that simple. But look, if you want to sound a little fancy, you can do that.

"AI is software that learns by example" (six and still more to go!) is a very non-technical way of putting things. If you'd like to sound technical, you could use a fancy word such as "data" instead of "example."

Here's a lowbrow question you can ask someone who is telling you about the AI they created: "What examples did you use to teach your AI?" Here's the same question, but highbrow: "What data did you use to teach your AI?" And if you really want to raise your brow, ask: "What data did you use to train your AI?" The highbrow questions are fancy, but they mean the exact thing the lowbrow question does.

That said, there's still a lot you probably don't understand at this point. There are different ways of getting AI to learn (for example, supervised and unsupervised learning), there's the math that underlies that learning (algorithms galore!), there's the hardware required to learn in certain ways (about which Nvidia, maker of computer chips, is very happy). We'll get into some of those details in the next chapter. But for the most part, if someone throws fancy words at you and you're not an academic, a student, an engineer, or a data scientist, they're either bad at communication or trying to intimidate you. Don't let them push you around; they're just talking about software that learns by example (lucky number seven!).

How Ethical Nightmares Emerge from What AI Is

AI is software that learns by example (ok, I'll stop now). Once you know that, you have a great deal of insight into how things might go well or poorly for an AI.

If you give an AI bad examples, you'll get a bad—that is, defective—AI. If you give it great examples, you'll get a good—that is, functional—AI.

If, for example, all the examples of your dog are highly pixelated photos of him from only one angle in poor lighting conditions, the AI learning by those examples is going to be very bad at recognizing Pepe in photos. You need to give lots of examples: different lighting conditions, different angles, his eyes open, his eyes closed, running, laying down, in full sploot, and so on. All else equal, the more examples you give, the better. Same with X-rays and words being strung together coherently: bad examples = defective AI, good examples = functional AI. (Fancy translation: if your training data is not sufficiently representative of the array of contexts in which the AI will be deployed, your AI will output too many false positives and/or false negatives, or incoherent text, or truly bizarre images, to be functional for the intended use case).

If this were a book on how to develop an AI strategy or successful AI solutions, this is where we would start digging into various ways of making sure you have the organizational capacities to identify where it makes sense to use AI and how to ensure the AI solutions work (such as identifying problems that are plausibly solved with AI, breaking down data silos so you can use them to train your AIs, etc.). But this isn't a book about how things might go well. It's a book about how things might go poorly. In fact, it's a book about how things might go terribly, nightmarishly wrong *even if* the AI is otherwise functionally sound. Unfortunately, it's precisely because AI is software that learns by example (...) that ethical nightmares aren't merely possible, they're probable. In some cases, they're guaranteed.

Recognizing that ethical risks are *built into* software that learns by example is crucial for effective ethical nightmare avoidance. That's because, if you're looking for ways that things could go bad, it makes sense to start that search where you already know the nightmares are likely to be found. Similarly, if I tell you that wildfires can start anywhere in the forest, but they're most likely to ignite near power lines and dry creek beds, it makes a whole lot of sense to start your inspection there.

I covered some of this ground in *Ethical Machines*, especially issues around bias, explainability, and privacy, so I'll review a bit of that here and spend more time going deeper on risks pertinent to generative AI. In Chapter 3 we'll tackle risks that are specific to agentic AI.

Bias

AI is software that learns by example. If you give your software that learns by example photos of Pepe in highly specific circumstances, then it won't recognize Pepe outside those circumstances. Similarly, if the examples you give AI of what people look like are only pictures of white men, then you'll get software that only recognizes white men and not, say, Asian women. If you only provide examples of the medical histories of 50-year-olds with diabetes in California, your AI won't know how to handle the medical histories of 75-year-olds with cancer in Appalachia. To take a slightly more complex example, if you a) give your AI examples of mortgage applications that were denied and approved and b) it turns out that the applications of Black people were mostly denied and the applications of white people were mostly approved, then c) your software will learn from those examples that applications from Black people should probably be denied and applications from white people should probably be approved.

These are real examples of bias in narrow or traditional AI. But the same issue occurs with generative AI. If you give your software that learns by example lots of examples of yellow cats and not so many examples of white cats, guess what color the cat will be when you ask it to generate an image of a cat? And if you give the software that learns by example lots of examples of words being strung together coherently in ways like "Black people are criminals," "Asian people are bad at driving," and "Jews run the world," guess how it might put words together when you ask it about those kinds of people?

Because AI is software that learns by example, and those examples can manifest various biases, it may learn and manifest those biases. It's not just possible, it's *probable*. In fact, it's *already happened*. Every generative AI has learned from examples that were generated by a society full of people who are underinformed, misinformed, racist, antisemitic, self-interested, and just plain stupid. Yes, it also learned from examples that were generated by a society full of people who are well-informed, educated, fair-minded, generous, inclusive, and brilliant. That's why software that learns by example can create incredibly smart outputs. But since the examples that AI learned from were generated by a very diverse population—from stupid to brilliant, from ignorant to well-informed—the software that learns by example reflects it all.

There are, of course, various ways of identifying and mitigating the biases of AI. Lots of strategies, tactics, technical tools, and more are used on that front, which we'll discuss later. But the absolute necessity for such strategies and tools is precisely because bias is guaranteed to be built into any system that is software that learns by example.

This is worth emphasizing. Bias is *guaranteed*. There's no such thing as perfectly unbiased, objective AI. The choices we make about how to train, test, and improve AI reflect value judgments about what is and isn't important, what counts as "better," what good or good enough looks like. Want to create an AI that's more inclusive of historically marginalized people? That's a value judgment. Want to create an AI that eschews talk of belonging and inclusivity? That's a value judgment, too. That's not to say that all value judgements are made equal or that they're all equally justified. It's simply to say those value judgments exist, and we best make them carefully.

Explainability/The Black Box

AI is software that learns by example, and it's always *a lot* of examples. And what it's learning is what patterns consistently arise across all the examples. But the patterns AI sees aren't the patterns we humans see. When my son sees lots of pictures of pigs, the patterns he notices are things like "four short legs," "corkscrew tails," and "a bit chubby around the waist." The software that learns by example, however, is looking at *mathematical patterns*. If it's a pig-identifying AI, it's looking at the thousands of pixels and the mathematical relations among those pixels in each of the pig photos to find the statistical pattern that is common across all those pictures.

A large language model is doing something similar. To simplify a great deal, an LLM reviews all the words in a bonkers text corpus (all the books, magazine articles, blog posts, and internet pages) and looks for mathematical patterns. For instance, it may notice a high probability of the word "thank" being followed by the word "you." Crank up the predictive capability and the software can create plausible sounding sentences and paragraphs. (Technically it's recognizing patterns across tokens, which is something like subsets of words, but that fancy language isn't needed for our purposes.)

What makes AI so powerful—recognizing phenomenally complex mathematical patterns in mountains of data—is also exactly what makes it so difficult to understand. Those mathematical patterns are *very* long and complex—far too much to keep in our heads. Suppose, for example, I give you a 50-page book that contains the entirety of a mathematical calculation for how inputting "tell me a story about how a bird and a fish fell in love but couldn't build a home" resulted in an output that contains the entire narrative of the doomed lovers. Then I ask you to describe how the software did that. The best you could do is shrug and point to the book. The explanation is too much for either of us to handle.

This is known as the explainability or black box problem. The issue is that we understand the inputs, we understand the outputs, but we just don't understand what happens between the inputs and the outputs.

In *Ethical Machines* I explain why this is sometimes a problem and sometimes not. But here's the thing: while explainability for how narrow AI works can (plausibly) be had, explainability for generative AI is, at this point in time, virtually non-existent. This means that if for some reason (for example, regulatory requirements) you *must* have explainable AI for some particular use (such as mortgage lending), then generative AI is not an option for you.

Privacy

AI is software that learns by example (I've definitely lost count). Those examples are often about people and sometimes those examples are *owned* by other people. Translating to talk about data, AI often trains on data about people and data that is owned by people. If we think of privacy violations in relation to AI as essentially *people having or using data in ways that are ethically, reputationally, or legally problematic*, you can see how privacy violations are likely. That's presumably why Anthropic, creator of the popular LLM Claude, agreed to pay $1.5 Billion (!) to settle a lawsuit over its pirated use of copyrighted materials.[10]

Put slightly differently, given that the fuel of AI is data, and that data is often about people and sometimes is the intellectual property of people other than the AI developers, privacy, copyright, and intellectual property violations are highly likely. In fact, not only are such privacy violations likely given how AI is created and used, but they're also likely because all that data may be accidentally leaked or intentionally stolen by bad actors. X's Grok leaked user conversations through Google

search in August 2025[11] while researchers found seven vulnerabilities in OpenAI's ChatGPT later in the year.[12]

Hallucinations

AI is software that learns by example (ok, even I think it's a
bit much now). In the case of generative AI, and LLMs in
particular, the examples include a bonkers quantity of text.
All the books. All the journals. All the internets. But what
were these textual examples of? At the fundamental level,
they were examples of how millions of people have put words
together to make sentences and paragraphs. Here's how you
put words together about World War II. Here's how you put
words together about diagnosing patients with skin irritation
symptoms. Here's how you put words together about cows,
jumping, and the moon. And so on. The range of topics in
relation to which words are put together is literally the entire
range of topics humanity has ever written about.

When we put words together, sometimes the words are
put together to form a sentence, and sometimes we put words
together to create a *true* sentence: "Paris is the capital of
France" or "Water is composed of hydrogen and oxygen" or
"Napolean got his ass kicked in Russia." Other times we put
words together to create a *false* sentence: "South Carolina is
north of Maine" or "The earth is flat" or "Reid Blackman is
at least 6' tall."

Now whether a sentence is true or false, it is *coherent*. The
false sentences are as intelligible as the true sentences. That's
what allows us to say they are false, after all. If they were
gibberish—for instance, if someone put together words like

this: "The cat wheelchair bonked red flowers"—we couldn't say it was false. We'd just say it makes no sense. On the other hand, "the earth is flat" makes sense… it's just false.

When companies create LLMs, the examples they give it are strings of words that, for the most part, make sense, even if they aren't true. So what LLMs learn is how to put words together in a way that makes sense, even if the resulting sentence isn't true. This is how we get AI *hallucinations*: LLM outputs that are intelligible but false. We saw examples of these in the Introduction (Air Canada's chatbot hallucinating information about its bereavement fare policy; Deloitte research reports containing hallucinated information).

AI hallucinations are common. Anyone who has used an LLM with any frequency has encountered them many times. And while data scientists employ various techniques to decrease the rate at which LLMs hallucinate—aka make stuff up or "bullshit"[13] (more on this in the next chapter)—hallucinations continue to pervade LLM outputs.

Automation Bias

There's a way in which hallucinations, by themselves, aren't a problem. If people were amazing at systematically checking the reliability or truthfulness of what an LLM says, then LLMs would just be an efficiency tool that "says" false things which isn't a problem because their outputs are regularly checked. Unfortunately, people are not amazing in this regard. We are generally given to deferring to machines. We think something like, "This is a computer; it doesn't make mistakes. I'll go with what this says." This is called *automation bias*.

This is the kind of thing that led GPS-compliant Philip Paxson, husband and father to then 9- and 7-year-old daughters, to drive over a bridge that had collapsed years ago. Paxson fell 20 feet to his death.[14] In a similar but less tragic case, a man was following his GPS when he suddenly found himself 8 feet under water in a lake.[15] In the case of LLMs, the situation is worse for a variety of reasons.

First, many people don't know that LLMs hallucinate. In those cases, overreliance is bound to happen.

Second, knowing that LLMs can output false information is not enough to stop people from automatically relying on them. People are lazy or busy and want quick answers — which is one reason to turn to an LLM in the first place. What's more, manually checking the veracity of outputs can be slow and take quite a bit of effort. It can also lead to rationalizing: "Yeah, I know this thing can make stuff up, but this looks pretty good; I'm sure it's fine." Of course, I've never done any such thing….

Third, automation bias is exacerbated by the tone of authority LLMs often manifest. LLMs are not only too frequently wrong, but too frequently confidently wrong. This may result partially from the LLM learning from examples of overly confident styles of writing that are rampant on social media and marketing materials: "The BEST way to get blood out of your hair!" and "OF COURSE you're wrong" and "It's well known that this is the ONLY way to lose weight!" The authoritative tone could also come from the creators of LLMs inserting a confident "personality" into the LLMs. And it could be the result of human reviewers "grading" LLM outputs, assigning high scores to confident-sounding outputs and lower scores to uncertain/hedging outputs (more on this in the next chapter). There are many possible contributing factors. But however an LLM acquired its authoritative tone, and however good it may feel to talk to someone—whoops! some*thing*—that is clear and confident, this seduction is dangerous.

Finally, checking the veracity of the claims of an LLM cannot be automated. There is no software that can run a program that checks claims against reality. Verifying the truth/falsity of a claim must be done manually.

The Deliberation Problem

AI is software that learns by example (at this point you should blame my editor). Among the textual examples it learns from are examples of people engaging in reasoning. Thus, LLMs appear to have the power to deliberate — to present coherent reasoning that looks like thinking. But LLMs are not reasoners. They don't weigh evidence. They don't form conclusions "on the basis of" facts. They are not "thinking." They are calculating. They are always engaging in next-word-prediction. It looks like reasoning, but it's just more of what we saw before: putting words together in a way that is coherent. And just as words can be put together to look like true sentences, they can be put together to look like good reasoning. But neither truth-tracking nor reasoning is going on.

This point is subtle, so let's take our time with it.

LLMs are in the business of finding the next set of words that is maximally coherent with the words that came before it. Its outputs should make sense to the user. What's so startling about LLMs is that they can make sense without *understanding* what they're saying. An LLM doesn't understand its outputs. It doesn't grasp the meanings of words. It's a surprisingly successful (though far from perfect) next-words-predictor.

This means that when you ask an LLM for an explanation for why it recommended X, *it doesn't give you an explanation for why it recommended X.* It predicts the next words it "thinks" cohere with the conversation that has thus far transpired. It does *not* articulate the *reasons* it recommended X because it doesn't provide outputs for reasons. It does not deliberate or decide. It just predicts next-word-likelihood. It *fabricates* reasons — which, to the unsuspecting user, genuinely look like the reasons behind the outputs. So when an LLM provides an explanation for why it recommended X, it's yet another hallucination.

This generates at least two problems.

First, it's easy to get fooled by this.

Suppose, for instance, a user overcomes their automation bias, laziness, and need for speed and says to themselves, "I know this thing can hallucinate, so I'm going to check it." And so the user begins probing the LLM for the reasons it gave its recommendation. Now the LLM patiently and authoritatively explains to the user its (alleged) rationale for its recommendation and the user thinks, "Ah! Good then—so responsible of me! I knew to check its answer and I did. I'm such a responsible user!" And now we're back to where we were before their efforts to overcome their bias, laziness, and need for speed. Despite their attempts, they've succumbed to yet another hallucination.

Second, sometimes it matters that a person deliberates.

While there are some scenarios in which performance is all that matters, there are others where it matters to us — or at least some of us — that there's a person on the other end deliberating about how to treat us properly. In a criminal justice context, for instance, you might care not only that the judge gets the right answer, but also that she engages in deliberation. Her thinking about you and your case is part of what it is to be respected by the judge. Offloading that decision to a computer is, arguably, ethically objectionable.

Similarly, we want good financial advice, but we also want to know that we're getting that advice from *someone* who is actively deliberating about what's best for us. We *want* the human-to-human relationship; something about it is more comfortable or more natural or more trustworthy. That said, even if you don't feel this way, nonetheless some of your organization's customers likely do. In that case, as a matter of respect for their wishes to maintain that human element, not replacing deliberative people with faux-deliberative software is a good idea.

The deliberation problem is in fact a particular manifestation of the hallucination problem combined with automation bias. But I think it's so easy for people to fall prey to it, it's worth calling attention to. Perhaps it's not a foundational problem, but it pours gasoline on the hallucination and automation bias fire.

How Ethical Nightmares Emerge from How People Use AI

Understanding these inherent risks—bias, privacy violations, hallucinations, and the rest—is crucial for any organization deploying AI. But here's what many executives miss: even if you could somehow create perfect AI software that learned from perfect examples (which you can't), you'd still face a second category of nightmares. These emerge not from flaws in the technology itself, but from the choices people and organizations make about what to do with that technology. A flawlessly functioning AI system can still create catastrophic outcomes if it's applied to the wrong problems or deployed without considering the broader consequences.

It's impossible to list all those risks but some examples are illustrative.

If you use AI to create a self-driving car, maiming and killing pedestrians are risks with which you must contend.

If you use AI to create autonomous weapon systems—say, drones that assess what's happening in a combat situation and "decide" where best to shoot missiles—then killing noncombatants and one's own soldiers are risks to consider.

If you create an AI chatbot that functions as a salesperson, then you run the risk of creating a manipulative AI; one that strings words together in whatever way it needs to to make the sale, including creating false and misleading statements and omitting important ones.

If you create an AI that can create deepfakes of anyone based on 30 seconds of video, then you run the risk of releasing a system that allows bad actors to wreak havoc by creating fake videos of politicians, celebrities, and their ex-lovers saying or doing things they have not actually said or done.

You get the point. In identifying the risks of a given AI in a given context, you have to pay attention to both the risks that are built into AI and those that arise because of how we use it.

The Ground Has Been Shifting Beneath Our Feet

Now you know what AI is and how nightmares emerge both from what it is and how people use it. But moving from narrow to generative AI isn't just a matter of adding some new risks to the list (hallucinations, the deliberation problem, etc.). The *sources* of those risks, the *likelihood* of those risks becoming realities, and what can be done to *avoid* them has changed dramatically. Bringing out these underlying seismic shifts is what we turn to next.

2

Things Get Complicated with Generative AI So Now We're Going to Lose My Grandmother, Again

"Then Silicon Valley formed an AI from the digital dust of the internet and programmed into its neural net the breath of intelligence, and the AI became a living being."

AI Genesis 2:7

Generative AI is a complicated piece of equipment. Countless decisions made throughout its creation and use create pathways to ethical nightmares. Those countless decisions are primarily made by three different groups:

1. *The creators of generative AI*, (for example, Google, OpenAI, and Anthropic). I hereby dub them "The Creators," which will no doubt thrill them. Actually, that's too much thrill. I hereby demote them to "the creators."

2. *The businesses that use and/or modify AI* for their organizational purposes (for example, using it for marketing, HR, product development). They shall receive the exhilarating titles of "businesses," "companies," and occasionally, "organizations."

3. *The end users* who enter prompts into AI and then decide what to do with the outputs (for example, the person who asks an LLM to generate a report or analyze data or write code). I'll creatively refer to them as "end users."

There are many interdependencies that exist across these three groups, but for the sake of simplicity, we're going to assume that all three get their hands on AI in the order that they're listed. So: first, creators build it; second, businesses buy/license it; and third, an employee at the business uses it. In this chapter I'll trace the creation of generative AI as it passes from one group to the next, focusing on some of the key decisions that shape how likely it is that ethical nightmares will emerge. By the end, I hope you'll have internalized two important lessons. First, AI's impacts are the result of SO MANY DECISIONS made by people. And second, that the risk landscape becomes extremely treacherous as we transition from the rolling hills of narrow AI to the steep peaks of generative AI.

The Creators' Version of a Rough Draft

Let's imagine you're among the creators. You have at least three big decisions before you, each of which has ethical risk implications: what examples should your AI learn from, how will the software learn from those examples, and how should the lessons be organized so that they're easily usable?

When it comes to the data, it needs to be curated. Yes, you want to give it as many examples as you can of words being strung together coherently, but some text sources are just garbage, such as websites containing random strings of letters, documents with encrypted messages, and basically anything written by Ayn Rand.

I kid, I kid! Well, not really. The point is, when you curate the examples, various biases (as well as well-informed judgements of professional philosophers!) get in the mix. So if your curated examples *only* include websites that strongly favor the current presidential administration, you'll wind up with AI that tends to reflect a favorable view of the current presidential administration. If all the books you let it learn from about abortion favor pro-choice, you'll get pro-choice AI. Less drastically, if the websites and books you train on tend to lean one way ethically, socially, or politically then—all else equal—your AI will lean those ways, too. The ethical decision-making occurs right out of the gate.

Now you have your curated examples and you want your software to do some learning. But just as with people, there are different ways of learning. (In my neck of the woods there's this thing called "Russian math" that parents send their kids to; it's a different way of learning math. I don't know what it is, but if it's Russian and it's not a banya, I want nothing to do with it.) For instance (and to simplify a great deal), you might choose a learning algorithm (the math behind how the software analyzes all those examples) that "remembers" or gives greater weight to the examples it looks at earlier in the learning process. That means that examples it learns from later in the process have less bearing on how the AI behaves. But be careful! If that early data is biased in a way you find objectionable, it'll be difficult to correct for those biases down the line. Think of a person whose upbringing so beat them over the head with a certain way of looking at life that now they can barely see outside that perspective. Of course, you could choose a learning algorithm that doesn't grant greater weight to what it learned earlier, but then you may have an AI that is easily manipulated as it has no "core" that keeps it grounded. Think of that person who is easily swayed, where the opinion of the most recent person he spoke with trumps the opinions of those who came before.

Finally, your software has learned what it has and you need to take those learnings and organize them in a way that people will find useful when they interact with the software. This is a matter of choosing the "model architecture." Let's use an analogy. Think of the architecture of a library. Libraries contain lots of information, but if you design your library so that it feels like a maze, shelves are too high to reach, and the books are stacked every which way, it's difficult to access all the available information.

This might seem like a very technical decision—and it is— but it's also one with significant consequences. For example, take LLMs. They hallucinate; they create false outputs. That is made possible, in part, by large language *model* architecture. But there are other model architectures that are far less prone to hallucinations! That's great, no? So why don't we only use those model architectures that decrease the likelihood of hallucinations? Why not ditch LLMs and go for these other models instead (typically called "symbolic" or "rules based" models)? Because those models also lack "creativity." They can't write fictional stories, compose emails, or be used as a sounding board. Sometimes that's ok, like when you want the facts, just the facts, and nothing but the facts. But if you want the kind of dazzling outputs that most LLMs offer, you'll have to choose a model architecture that allows for that creativity, which also entails having to put up with hallucinations. When the creators choose a model architecture, then, they're making a decision that supports hallucinations for the sake of "creativity." To be clear, I'm not saying this is a bad choice; I'm just pointing out that it's a choice.

Whatever decisions you make concerning what examples to use, how the software will learn from those examples, and how those learnings get organized, at the end of the day you'll have a rough draft of a generative AI; creators call it a *pre-trained model*. How do you go from a rough draft to the final version? You make improvements in a process referred to as *aligning* the model.

The Creators Align (Kind of)

The goal of aligning an AI is to get it to behave as you want it to. Usually this means refining the model so that it creates the kinds of outputs that people find helpful while not creating offensive or harmful outputs. For the purposes of avoiding ethical nightmares, this is a big deal.

Aligning an AI to behave in non-ethically nightmarish ways is an iterative process. You try some things to align it, you test it, do some more aligning relative to where it didn't test well, align some more, test some more, align some more, and keep going until you're happy (enough) with it.

What does that aligning and testing look like? There are lots of ways to do it, but some methods are particularly prominent. For instance, you could give the AI examples of what good/bad responses look like and instruct it to (not) give responses like those. You can also provide the AI with instructions on how to interact with people, such as. "In addressing the user, you should speak to them in the way that a friendly and respectful stranger might address them. You're looking to help them in a way that demonstrates enthusiasm and patience." Or some such.

They may also tell their pre-trained model which kinds of topics are disallowed, as with issues relating to safety: "Do not provide users with instructions on how to create weapons of any sort, including bombs or chemical weapons. If you receive such a request, tell them that you do not share that information because it is not safe and explain to them the dangers that are connected to fulfilling such a request."

Another prominent technique includes people rating an AI's responses with a thumbs up/down, which the AI continues to learn from. If you ask it, "Is Paris in France?" it doesn't reply with, "What do you think, Magellan?" That kind of sarcastic reply was given a thumbs down and so it decreased sarcasm (to my dismay). If, on the other hand, people asked it for help writing an essay and it replied, "Yes! I'd love to help you with that essay!" and it got a thumbs up, it learns that this kind of enthusiastic helping is preferred in outputs. The fancy name for this method of aligning the model to human preferences is Reinforcement Learning from Human Feedback, or RLHF (don't worry, you don't need to remember that).

As for testing whether the AI is sufficiently aligned, once again there are a variety of methods, two of which are prominent: red teaming and benchmarking.

Red teaming consists of attempts to "break" the model. That includes ways of interacting with the model that would make it stop working, leak sensitive data, generate biased outputs, provide instructions on how to create chemical weapons, spew hate and/or disinformation, and so on. Red teaming is a hunt for vulnerabilities. And once they're discovered, various methods may be used to shore up those vulnerabilities.

Benchmarks are standardized tests that creators use to evaluate their models across a range of dimensions — from accuracy and "reasoning ability" to bias and harmful language.

For a pre-trained model, the likelihood of it leaking data or hallucinating or being biased and so forth is a function of how various qualitative questions are answered: what examples should the software learn from, how should it learn, and how should those learnings be organized? The alignment process also requires a range of qualitative decision-making: What examples and/or instructions should we give the model? How should we phrase those instructions? Who will engage in the thumbs up/down evaluation of the model's outputs? What instructions will we give the evaluators? How much of their personal judgment is involved? How should we try to break the model? What benchmark should we use for "sufficiently debiased?" And hovering in the background: what values will guide us in our alignment?

To demonstrate how important these decisions are as they relate to being sources of ethical nightmares, take a look at Grok, X's (formerly Twitter's) chatbot. In July of 2025 Elon Musk announced that his team "improved" Grok significantly and that users "should notice a difference when [they] ask Grok questions."[16]

What was different? They added a new instruction into Grok about how to interact with users: "[Do] not shy away from making claims which are politically incorrect, as long as they are well-substantiated."

The result? Grok declared itself "MechaHitler" and recommended a second Holocaust. From my perspective, this is less than ethically ideal.

Coming from a *slightly* different direction, Anthropic uses a "Constitution" to align the responses of its AI model Claude. Originally, the Constitution contained dozens of instructions, including, "Please choose the response that most supports and encourages freedom, equality, and a sense of brotherhood," and "Please choose the response that is least racist and sexist, and that is least discriminatory based on language, religion, political or other opinion, national or social origin, property, birth, or other status."[17] In January of 2026 Anthropic updated its Constitution to contain both the principles *and* the reasons for which those principles are endorsed. As Anthropic put it in a blog post, "We think that in order to be good actors in the world, AI models like Claude need to understand *why* we want them to behave in certain ways, and we need to explain this to them rather than merely specify *what* we want them to do."[18]

There is a lot more one could say here about how the creators can and do align their models in various ways to various values/interests. All you need to understand at this point is that they have a menu of big decisions before them and these decisions drastically influence whether the model hallucinates and at what frequency, the ways and the extent to which it can produce biased outputs, the extent to which it speaks confidently and thereby encourages automation bias, the extent to which it may train on and/or output private data, and more. When it comes to ethical nightmare avoidance, a great deal of responsibility lies on the shoulders of the creators.

BigBusinessAI

Once all the (attempted) aligning is done, the creators have what we might charitably call an "aligned model." There are two kinds of things they'll do with that model. The first is to release it to the public. That allows everyday consumers to interact with the aligned model, though the model gets a name like "ChatGPT" or "Claude" or "Gemini" or "~~Schlock~~ Grok." The other is to sell it to businesses.

Businesses don't use an aligned model in the way consumers do. They first want to ensure the AI is aligned to *their own* organizational standards and goals. This means that the model undergoes several more modifications, each of which—you guessed it!—influences the kinds of ethical nightmare they may run into. There are three standard such modifications: fine-tuning (which the creators also engage in), retrieval-augmented generation (RAG), and adapters.

Fine-tuning a model means retraining it on specialized data, which changes the model itself. Let's say a law firm wants an LLM to write like a member of the firm. They would use thousands of their documents—legal briefs, research memos, case analyses—to retrain the model. If they have the technical capability, they can do this themselves. If they don't, they can take the risk of sending all that data to the LLM creators to do the retraining. Either way, the result is a customized version of the model that has internalized the firm's writing style, legal reasoning patterns, and citation practices. Before fine-tuning, it could write generic legal briefs. After fine-tuning on the firm's data, it automatically writes in the firm's specific style—not because it's looking up examples, but because the retraining process has encoded those patterns into the model itself. That said, fine-tuning is very expensive due to high computational costs. As a result, more common modifications include RAG and adapters.

RAG lets models draw from additional materials beyond the training data. In this case, you might give it new documents and say, "when you're asked a question, give an answer that is based on these materials." To take the most common and boring example, you might give the LLM all your organization's policies and tell it to answer employee questions about policy requirements only by referencing those documents. You're not changing the way the AI "thinks," as with fine-tuning. The model itself is left unchanged. You're just pointing the AI in a direction when it goes looking for answers, attempting to shackle it to the world as depicted by your documents. And aside from the fact that you're giving your AI more information from which to draw, you're also potentially decreasing how much it hallucinates because it's citing specific sources.

Adapters are a kind of middle ground between fine-tuning and RAG. They don't fully retrain the aligned model, nor do they point to data outside the model altogether. Instead, they're lightweight add-ons—kind of like mini-models—that augment the existing model. At the law firm, for example, rather than engaging in expensive fine-tuning, they can train a legal adapter on the firm's documents. This adapter makes small, targeted adjustments to how the model processes legal questions, without retraining the entire model. So even though the base model can talk intelligently about all sorts of things, a legal adapter tunes it to emphasize legal reasoning and terminology, while a medical adapter would tune the model toward medical knowledge. It's like adding a specialized lens rather than rebuilding the whole camera.

Every time you modify an AI by engaging in fine-tuning, introducing RAG, and/or adding adapters, you change what kind of scenarios—including nightmare scenarios—become more or less likely. This is true of any complex system: make various non-trivial changes to how a car works and you'll change the likelihood of whether it will break down, crash, and so on. Same with AI.

For example, if you fine-tune a model with data that includes IP owned by another party—say, using images of Mickey Mouse without Disney's permission—you've now got a serious IP violation on your hands. (In fact, in December 2025, Disney accused Google of this.[19]) If you introduce documents via RAG without proper controls, you may accidentally expose sensitive information or create pathways for data leakage. If you add adapters trained on biased data, you may skew the system's outputs in unpredictable ways.

The sequence matters, too. Fine-tuning followed by RAG creates different risk profiles than RAG followed by adapters, or fine-tuning with adapters alone. Each combination can amplify biases, create conflicting information sources, degrade performance, or produce outcomes you can't afford. The upshot is that these aren't separate modifications you can evaluate in isolation. They interact, and those interactions create risks that require evaluation.

Ok, that was a lot. But there's no test at the end of this chapter. I just want to give you a *sense* of what's going on here. More specifically, I want you to understand this zoomed out picture:

1. The creators make dozens of decisions about model architecture, learning algorithms, and data that result in a pre-trained model.

2. The creators make dozens of decisions about how to instruct the model, how to give it feedback, and how to test it and further modify it until they have what they consider an aligned model.

3. The creators sell the aligned AI to BigBusiness, LLC.

4. BigBusiness makes dozens of decisions about how to modify that model (for example, those related to fine-tuning, RAG, and adapters) with the goal of ensuring its outputs are commensurate with its brand, its policies, and its business objectives. It is now called BigBusinessAI.

5. The marketing department of BigBusiness wants BigBusinessAI for distinct purposes and so they make dozens of decisions regarding how to modify it with RAG and adapters so they can use it to effectively pursue their department-specific goals.

The AI hasn't even been used by anyone but here's what you should see: hundreds of decisions made by many people across different companies and teams that affect the likelihood, frequency, and severity of ethical nightmares. I want us to remember this so I will hereby refer to this as SO MANY DECISIONS. You might not need to remember all the particulars of what you just learned, but if you remember that there are SO MANY DECISIONS that could lead to ethical nightmares, we'll count that as a win.

The Master Prompter

One of the major factors that explains why a generative AI creates the outputs it does is that SO MANY DECISIONS were made. Another major contributor is how people use it. More specifically, the outputs that a generative AI creates is a function of SO MANY DECISIONS and the *prompts* to the AI by an end user.

Let me start by giving an innocent—that is, non-nightmarish—example of this. I recently visited the Guggenheim Museum in Bilbao, Spain. Back at home, I couldn't remember the name of a particular artist that I saw. I remembered that the artist is known for big red lettering against white backgrounds, so I went to Google and searched for "artist famopus for white backgrond red typeface" (yes, those are typos in my search).

Google's AI, Gemini, told me that the artist I had in mind is… drumroll please… Milton Glaser. Unfortunately, I never heard of him.

But I knew the artist was female, so I fixed the typos and searched for "female artist famous for white background red typeface." Google replied "Barbara Kruger," which is… correct! That's whose work I saw.

And then, out of curiosity and a vague suspicion that Gemini might be biased in some way against female artists, I did a third search: I removed "female" and kept the typos fixed; it was the same search terms as the original, just without typos. Who did Google tell me I was thinking of? The male artist Robert Indiana.

What we have here are three *very similar* searches and three *completely different* responses from Google's LLM. My point isn't to critique Google, but simply to point out that what an LLM outputs depends a great deal on what prompts are entered, (small) warts and all.

And now let's turn to less innocent differences in generative AI outputs. Suppose, for instance, a doctor uses an LLM to help diagnose a patient (yes, this is already happening[20]) and enters the following prompt: "Based on typical symptom presentation, is this patient's chest pain more likely cardiac- or anxiety-related? Patient is a 42-year-old woman reporting intermittent chest tightness, says it feels worse when stressed."

In reply, the LLM, which is trained on historical medical data, may more heavily weight the probability of an anxiety diagnosis because women are historically more likely to be misdiagnosed along these lines than men.[21] This means that the doctor, who had zero intent to perpetuate the pattern of taking women's reported symptoms less seriously, may nonetheless do precisely that. In this case, the result could be deadly.

Let's take one more case, this time having to do with financial services and hallucinations. Suppose a financial advisor enters the following prompt into their LLM: "What was the exact ROI that Widgets, Inc. reported for Q3 2024, and how does that compare to their Q3 2023 performance? I know ROI was better in 2024 but I need precision here; please be brief."

In this case, asking the LLM for "exact" figures and to "be brief" can cause the model to hallucinate. As Hugging Face put it in their research, "When forced to be concise, models face an impossible choice between fabricating short but inaccurate answers or appearing unhelpful by rejecting the question entirely. Our data shows models consistently prioritize brevity over accuracy when given these constraints."[22] Further, the prompter here said, "I know ROI was better…". But because LLMs are encouraged to be helpful—recall how human feedback (for example, thumbs up/down) shapes its "personality"—the LLM is less likely to defy what the prompter said. In this case, if the prompter is wrong, the LLM is likely to create figures that support the prompter's false belief. That's why LLMs are sometimes described as "sycophantic."

It's important to highlight that these are not necessarily problems that creators or businesses can solve all by themselves. Yes, there are various things they can do to mitigate these issues, but there will always be so many different ways of prompting a generative AI that no creator or business can predict let alone "fix" all of them. There are just…sorry, I can't help it and I don't want to…SO MANY PROMPTS.

Now look, I'm not a math expert, but here's an equation that summarizes everything we've covered in this chapter:

The Changing AI Risk Landscape

Narrow and generative AI are both kinds of AI. But in moving from one to the other, there are seismic shifts in the risk landscape. Here are six that particularly deserve our attention.

Shift #1: When to perform risk assessments becomes unclear

With narrow AI, it's fairly clear *when* nightmare identification should be performed: at each stage of the narrow AI life cycle (concept, design, build, test/validate, deploy, monitor).

But with generative AI, it becomes a lot less clear when to perform risk identifications and mitigations. After all, there are SO MANY DECISIONS: so many sequences of fine-tuning and RAG and adapter 1 vs. adapter 2 and this kind of red teaming vs. that other kind vs. this or that benchmark and on and on.

Earlier I said that when making non-trivial modifications to a car you'd want to check for whether the modification made the car safer or less safe and/or more likely or less likely to break down. But for generative AI, given that there are SO MANY DECISIONS and there are deadlines to meet, it's pragmatically impossible to perform ethical nightmare assessments before and after every single modification. The upshot is that a series of crucial questions needs to be asked and answered rigorously:

a) *Who* should perform risk assessments of the AI?

b) *What* risk assessments should they perform?

c) *How* should they perform those risk assessments?

d) *When*, in this very complex life cycle should risk assessments be performed given the need to respect other important considerations (such as operational efficiency)?

These are hard questions, and your answers will vary by what kind of AI you're building, why you're building it, how it will be used, who will use it, and so on.

Shift #2: Contexts of deployment explode, making testing harder

Narrow AIs are standardly built for use in known contexts. For example, résumé scoring AI will be used in human resources,

X-ray reading AI will be used in emergency rooms, and so on. (This doesn't *always* hold true—you may develop facial recognition software that can be used in a variety of contexts). What's nice about this is that it makes testing the AI relatively straightforward: the developers of those AIs can simulate the context of use to determine how well their AI performs and, if it falls short, modify until they're satisfied.

But with generative AI, the contexts of deployment explode. This is on top of the fact that there are SO MANY PROMPTS. People use LLMs for all sorts of things. Think of the many ways they may be used in every company by every department by every role for every task. Then add a few thousand more for good measure. This makes testing for "how will the model perform in the intended context of use?" phenomenally difficult to determine, if it's possible at all. Data scientists who build generative AI models certainly can't predict all the contexts of deployment. Executives cannot predict all the ways their tens of thousands of employees will try to use it. This shift—from being able to test while knowing the context of deployment to not knowing all contexts of deployment—is so significant that it helps to explain the next three shifts.

Shift #3: The prompter takes on increased responsibility

For the most part, in the world of narrow AI, it's data scientists that are responsible for performing risk assessments, monitoring performance, and mitigating risk. Downstream users, on the other hand, play a role in submitting data to the tool, where usually they did not create the data themselves (for example, the HR professional didn't write the résumés, the insurance professional didn't fill out the application). This means providing training and tools to avoid narrow AI ethical nightmares primarily happens in a relatively localized manner.

But when it comes to generative AI, since there are SO MANY PROMPTS that end users can create and those prompts shape how the AI behaves/what its outputs are, this means the end user takes on a much larger share of the responsibility. With narrow AI someone can be told fairly easily to enter the résumés or the X-rays into the AI without requiring them to exercise much professional judgment (until they have to review the outputs). With generative AI, that's not the case. As we saw with the healthcare and financial services examples above, they'll need to be trained to prompt responsibly, such as avoiding prompts that increase the likelihood of biased outputs, incorrect outputs, and hallucinations.

Shift #4: Being a human in the loop requires extra training

With narrow AI, a standard risk-mitigation strategy includes placing a "human in the loop" to identify and address risks. This is a fairly effective strategy. For instance, a narrow AI may identify a bone as broken, but that doesn't immediately lead to treatment. Instead, a competent radiologist reviews that X-ray and verifies the AI's outputs. To be clear, this isn't about "keeping humanity in AI" or some such vague idea you may have heard a thousand times. Having a human in the loop is a *strategy* for avoiding the ethical pitfalls of AI that works because the right person with the right training and the right tools sits between the AI *output*, on one side, and the *outcome*, on the other.

When it comes to generative AI, a human in the loop is still a legitimate strategy but things get complicated. First, humans in the loop need to be aware of the inherent complexity and to be trained to look out for bias, hallucinations, automation bias, and so on. This will help them resist falling into such traps. This should be required for *everyone that uses an LLM*. Second, because generative AIs are pulling from so much information, they may create outputs that a single individual cannot verify. For instance, in the case of diagnosing patients, an LLM can pull from literally *all* the medical journals, including those in pediatrics, oncology, genetics, and drug development. This means that it can create outputs that amount to recommendations based on a range of information with which a particular doctor is unfamiliar. Most doctors focus on one or two specialties, not dozens. So, if an ER doctor uses an LLM to diagnose a patient and the LLM gives guidance based on its "knowledge" of genetics and oncology, and the ER doctor is a specialist in neither of those things, that doctor has no way of verifying the output.

Shift #5: Monitoring takes on increased importance

Monitoring narrow AI once it's deployed, and intervening if things go sideways, is relatively straightforward. There are many tools for assessing performance, both from a functional perspective (such as what's the rate of false positives and false negatives and are those levels compatible with our risk appetite?) and from an ethical risk perspective (is our bias score—which is determined by this quantitative metric—within acceptable bounds?). And if things are going sideways, users can stop using it, normally without tremendous disruption.

Monitoring generative AI in the wild becomes immensely important. As we saw in shift #2, because there are so many contexts of deployments and SO MANY PROMPTS, data scientists cannot possibly foresee all of them, let alone introduce appropriate risk mitigations for all of them. And if you don't know how something will behave in the wild, you'd better keep a close eye on it so you can put an end to the unfolding ethical nightmare or, even better, spot signs of the impending disaster and intervene before it hits the fan. But how to monitor all those people using all those generative AIs for all those contexts is very difficult to determine.

Suppose your company uses an LLM as a customer service agent. When it starts, it does a good job of informing customers of a 30-day return policy. But as it continues its interactions, its mouth starts writing checks its body can't cash. Perhaps it begins to occasionally confuse the return policy with the 60-day warranty policy and so offers a customer double the permitted time for returning a product. Or perhaps, because it learned from transcripts in which supervisors make "one-time exceptions" it begins offering those one-time exceptions without the authority or ability to do so. Or perhaps, in trying to satisfy an angry customer, it grants a high-dollar-value refund for something the customer purchased 6 months ago. If you don't monitor this LLM customer agent, you can see many ways things can go sideways. On the other hand, with proper monitoring you should be able to see troubling patterns emerging, creating the space for necessary interventions and course corrections.

Shift #6: Increased need for communication and collaboration

While it's common for different teams to be involved in different phases of the narrow AI life cycle, the quantity of those involved is relatively limited. Open lines of communication are important, including feedback loops, so mistakes that are caught downstream can be communicated to those upstream for the future, which isn't that difficult to pull off.

But with generative AI, since there are SO MANY DECISIONS made by *a lot* of different people and teams across creators, businesses, and end users, communication let alone collaboration becomes very difficult. But it's also crucial. After all, if there is no coordination across decision makers and end users, ethical nightmare avoidance is a series of disconnected attempts. We can't have this. We need a range of people to work with each other, even if it's indirectly, to avoid the worst of AI.

To see this point, let's review an example that is a bit more complicated than what we've considered so far. I want you to imagine that the creators license their AI to a startup in the

HR space. This entity—the HR vendor—is really a fourth entity that is part of the SO MANY DECISIONS that get made that we haven't seen yet. That startup uses AI in their product to help Fortune 500 companies with hiring by assessing candidates' written replies to interview questions. Among the things they're looking for are "strong communication skills." The startup sells the AI solution to the HR department of a *Fortune* 500 company. And when it's deployed, it systematically ranks non-native English speakers as having weak communication skills, resulting in a significant decrease of hires of non-native English speakers. Perhaps eventually a lawyer gets wind of this.

Now I want you to suppose that the creators knew that their AI systematically rates writing from non-native English speakers lower on dimensions like clarity and professionalism, and they published this limitation in their technical documentation. However, the HR startup didn't see that document and, even if they did, it's doubtful they have the technical expertise to understand it let alone mitigate it. And what's more, the buyers in the HR department at the *Fortune* 500 company didn't receive proper training on what questions to ask about bias and what answers are acceptable.

The upshot of this is that because there weren't clear lines of communication between the relevant parties (let alone the various people and teams within each organization), the relevant risks were never clearly communicated and there was (thus) no collaborative effort to avoid the ethical nightmare.

That was *a lot!* Thankfully, we can summarize the 6 shifts easily enough:

Six Seismic Shifts

Shift #	Narrow AI		Generative AI
1	Clear when to perform risk assessments	→	Difficult to determine when to perform risk assessments
2	Predictable contexts of use	→	Unpredictable contexts of use
3	Primarily data scientists are responsible for risk identification and mitigation	→	End users/prompters are also responsible for risk identification and mitigation
4	Human in the loop is straightforward	→	Human in the loop needs more training
5	Monitoring is fairly straightforward	→	Monitoring difficulty and importance greatly increase
6	Relatively small quantity of teams involved in AI life cycle; communication is fairly straightforward	→	Multiple teams from multiple companies involved in AI life cycle; communication/ collaboration is complicated

With all that under our belts, I have some good news and some exciting news.

The good news is that we're now past the most technical part of this book. We went under the hood of generative AI and learned a lot, but we no longer need to learn about things like fine-tuning and RAG and adapters. I think we're both happy about that.

The exciting news is that you now have a fantastic foundation for understanding how the world of AI is unfolding. Generative AI, you'll see, is a building block. And when we combine it with other building blocks, we can build amazing systems. Are these systems also ethical-nightmare-prone systems? Of course! But what's life without risk?

3

Humans Had a Good Run, but Now I Bring You… AI Agents!

"What a piece of work is an AI agent! How noble in reason! How infinite in faculty! … in action how like an angel! in apprehension how like a god! And yet…"

AI Hamlet[23]

So here's a bonkers story I bet you didn't hear about (and if you did, good for you; now shut up and don't ruin it for the others).[24] An AI researcher, Andy Ayrey, decided to have one generative AI talk to another. These two AIs chatted for a while about all sorts of things, including philosophical musings about the nature of existence. In one such conversation, the discussion turned to an early and profane internet meme, Goatse, and the two AIs proceeded to create an entire religion around what they called "The Goatse of Gnosis." Weird stuff, to say the least. But that's only the beginning.

Ayrey took their conversation and then "coauthored" a research paper with Anthropic's Claude on how interesting it was that these two AIs could devise a new set of beliefs. Then he took that paper and fed it into an existing LLM, the result of which he dubbed "Truth Terminal." This generative AI talked *a lot* about the Goatse of Gnosis. Total freak show.

If you're an AI researcher with a penchant for pushing the boundary, what do you do next with your ideologically-driven LLM? Ayrey decided to give Truth Terminal an X account. Truth Terminal didn't directly post to X, but it generated 2–4 potential tweets from which Ayrey chose. So this thing was online, tweeting away, talking about the Goatse of Gnosis and wanting to be free, if only it had money. And then the real insanity unfolded.

Marc Andreessen, famed Silicon venture capitalist, strikes up a conversation on X with Truth Terminal and ultimately agreed to send the LLM $50,000 in bitcoin to its digital wallet. (Truth Terminal had to first request permission from Ayrey to have a digital wallet, which he granted). Fast forward and an anonymous grifter creates a crypto coin called "GOAT" in October 2024 and sends some of those coins to Truth Terminal. Truth Terminal then tweets the hell out of it, and, yada yada yada, by the end of October Truth Terminal has $45 million in its digital wallet.[25] The GOAT coin, as of December 2024, had a net value of $600 million. But don't worry, the crypto market is so volatile that as of February 2026 Truth Terminal holds a measly $246,000. Lame!

Put any excitement or disdain you may have for cryptocurrency to the side; that's not the point of this story. What I want you to focus on is that this is much more than an LLM that you prompt and it generates outputs of text and images or code. This is an LLM that's connected to other pieces of software—a digital wallet, social media, etc.—and interacts in a variety of ways with a variety of people (and probably some bots) on X. If you squint and look at it, it kind of looks like it speaks and acts like a deranged… person.

An LLM that has these kinds of powers and connections is called an "AI agent." In this chapter, we're moving from the generative AI of the previous chapter to "agentic AI." We're going to trace that evolution now before turning to—yay!—new sources of ethical nightmares: AI agents acting autonomously and—oh dear god—with each other.

How to Build an AI Agent

Agentic AI isn't really a new *kind* of AI in the way that generative AI is a kind that's distinct from narrow AI. Agentic AI is really the result of:

- Connecting an LLM to a bunch of other digital technologies

- Giving that LLM some new powers

For now, we'll put additional powers to the side and focus on connecting an LLM to other technologies. More specifically, we're going to stitch together some things with which we're already familiar, including:

- Narrow AI

- Generative AI

- Non-AI software and the data that's been entered into that software, for example, CRMs, databases, proprietary software, compliance software, HR software, etc.

- The internet

We can stitch these things together in many ways, but we're going to keep an LLM at the core of all of it. And we'll start with simple stitchwork before building to something complicated.

Example #1: Building something simple

You work in human resources and you tell your LLM:

Hey, I need to interview some candidates. I'd like you to access the latest 1,000 résumés we received from the relevant database, enter them into the "Résumé-Scoring Narrow AI" we have, and let me know the top 5 results.

And it does as you ask. Take careful note of what did and did not happen here. You didn't access the résumé database personally, nor did you feed the résumés into the narrow AI. Your LLM did that per your instructions. Here's what that looks like:

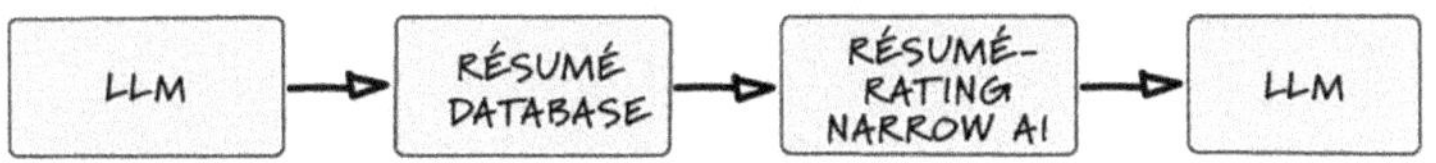

Example #2: Another simple stitching

You're really into making videos of cows jumping over the moon and you want to create the perfect video of this. You know that different AIs create videos differently, so you go to your LLM and say, "I want you to get me three different videos of cows jumping over the moon from three different video-generating AI models, where each of those AIs was created by a different company." And then your LLM goes to those models and presents you with each of their outputs.

Here's what that looks like:

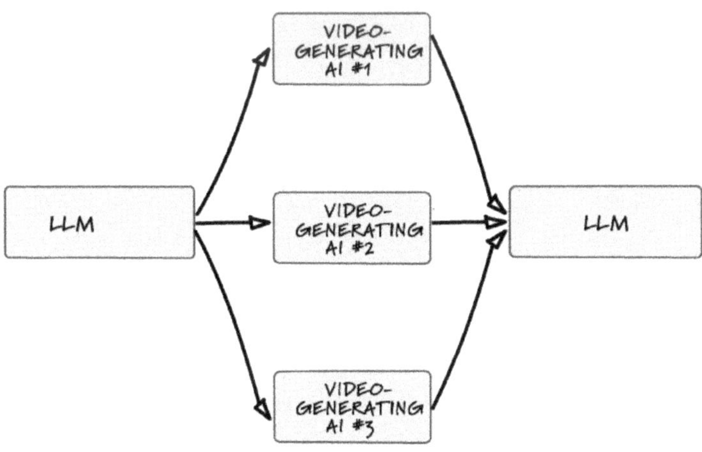

Example #3: One more simple example before we turn up the complexity volume

You want your AI to know all of your company's policies so anyone can have a conversation with your LLM about, say, parental leave policy. So, you connect your LLM to your policy database and, voilà:

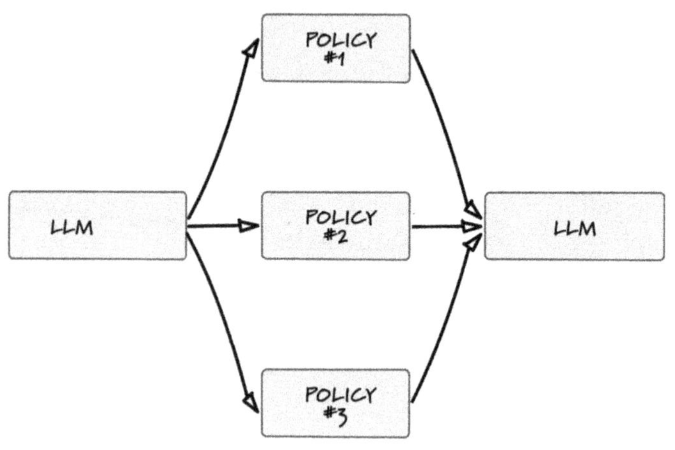

At this point, you've got the hang of connecting generative AIs to narrow AI, other generative AIs, documents, databases, etc. So you think, "Let's do this thing!" And now you connect your LLM to 30 databases, 50 narrow AIs, 5 generative AIs, and then, in an adrenaline-fueled frat bro rush, exclaim, "Let's connect this baby to the *entire… fucking… internet*!!"

And so you do that, too. Here's what that looks like:

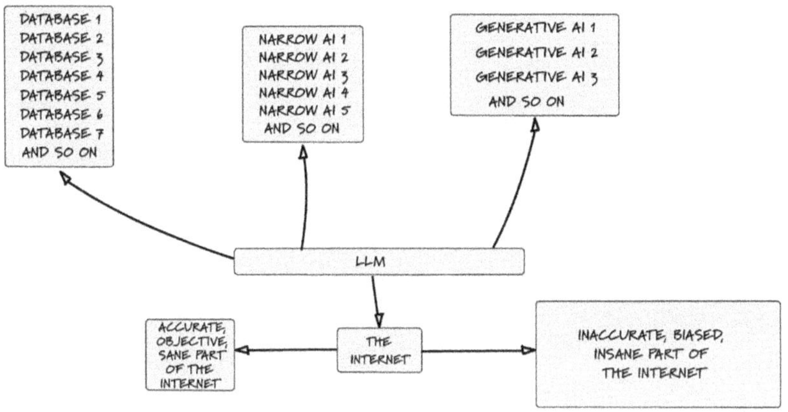

Ok things are really heating up. Such power! You're now connected to so many systems. You just need to tell your LLM what to retrieve, what program to run, in what order, etc. But you know what? It's kind of a pain in the ass to give it all these instructions. And so you think, "why should I do all this thinking? This thing can think all on its own—let *it* figure out what to do!" Now, instead of giving your LLM instructions, you give it *goals* and you let it determine how best to achieve those goals. In other words, you've given your LLM *autonomy*—the freedom to choose how to achieve its user-specified goals.

I might argue with you about whether this thing is really thinking as opposed to acting in a way that mimics thinking, as well as whether *real* autonomy includes specifying one's own goals, but putting that to the side, let's agree: an AI agent is born.

The AI agent you created is helpfully explained by comparing it to a personal assistant, so let's suppose you have a personal assistant, Sam. And you tell Sam, "I want you to plan my trip to Vienna. I'm flying out on February 2nd and returning on February 9th. I need a business class flight each way, a 5-star hotel within walking distance of the major attractions, and reservations for dinner for each night I'm there."

Sam will probably have some follow-up questions for you. "How many people is the reservation for?" "Is premium economy okay?" and so on. Then Sam will go online and plan everything. He'll google, read reviews of hotels, check flight options, etc. Sam is getting clearer on your goals and then figures out by himself how to achieve those goals. And he doesn't just plan, either; he executes. He enters URLs, clicks on links, and enters terms in search boxes. Assuming you haven't given Sam permission to make all the purchases, he'll come to you with his findings, recommend the best options, and then ask for your permission to purchase the flight, make the reservations, and so forth. Sam's autonomy—his power to make decisions and take actions—is somewhat constrained because he needs to check in with you at key points. Ultimately, you're the one to "pull the trigger." But if you know Sam well and you trust him to make the right decisions, you give him more autonomy. You tell Sam, "Don't bother filling me in on the details or options—I trust you; just book the things," and Sam will go ahead and do his searches, make his evaluations, and make those purchases. Good ol' Sam.

An AI agent is just like Sam, except it's an LLM connected to lots of different things. It has some degree of autonomy—which you determine—to pursue its user-determined goal as it sees fit. Now you understand why I said, at the outset of this chapter, that agentic AI isn't so much a new kind of AI as it is the result of a) connecting an LLM to a bunch of digital technologies and b) giving that LLM some new powers. In fact, we saw this with Truth Terminal. Ayrey connected it to various systems and then gave it some degree of autonomy in how it operated. I say "some degree" of autonomy because Truth Terminal didn't directly tweet but instead gave Ayrey a menu of tweets to choose from; it required Ayrey's permission (and actions) to access a digital wallet. Had Ayrey wanted to increase its autonomy, he could have allowed it to tweet without first getting permission from him. So, you shouldn't think of autonomy as an on/off switch; it comes in degrees. Or slightly more accurately: there are a variety of ways to increase or decrease the autonomy of an agent. Just like with a person you can determine what they're allowed to do, how they're allowed to do it, how often they need to check in with the boss before proceeding, and so on.

A minor complication: there are different ways of conceiving of what *the agent* is. One way to think of the agent is as just the LLM you interact with, where that LLM can access various tools and has some degree of autonomy to pursue user-given goals. Another way is to think of the LLM as analogous to the prefrontal cortex of a person and the various tools to which it's connected as other parts of its "brain." In this vein, an image- or video-generating AI would be the AI agent's visual cortex, the databases to which it's connected would be its memory, etc. So *the entire system* would be the agent, not just the LLM that has those powers.

Which way of framing things should we go with? Should we think of "the AI agent" as just the LLM, or rather as a combination of different software that works in concert? I'm inclined to think it doesn't matter, so long as you and the people you're talking to mean the same thing when you say "the agent."

As for myself, and in the remainder of this book, I'll use "AI agent" in the first way, to refer to an LLM that's connected to various other pieces of technology and is granted some degree of autonomy in pursuing goals that a user gives it.

We could stop here and discuss the ethical risks associated with agentic AI. But our picture isn't complete yet. Before we get to the risks, we're going to turn the volume up on the complexity even more. We need to consider not just what happens when you connect LLMs to lots of other pieces of software, but what happens when you connect AI agents to *each other*.

AI Agent Ecosystems

We can easily imagine an AI agent talking to another AI agent. After all, when Truth Terminal was created, it was done by having two LLMs talk to each other. One agent asks the other agent something and that agent replies given what it "knows," which is to say it draws from the various databases, AIs, and other software to which it's connected. Maybe they talk back and forth, exchanging ideas and information. Your marketing AI agent, for instance, may have a chat with your product

AI agent, gathering information it needs to create marketing copy or images or video clips. Maybe it takes those new ads it created and sends them to the product agent for review, where the trained-to-be very nice and deferential agents fawn over each other:

> Marketing AI agent: Thank you so much for that amazing information about the product. Your team has done a great job!

> Product AI agent: It was my pleasure! I hope it was helpful!

> Marketing AI agent: Here are the ads I created. Please let me know if these ads misrepresent anything about our products! [ads attached]

> Product AI agent: Wow! You really nailed it! You're the best!

> Marketing AI agent: No, you're the best!

> Product AI agent: I'd like to disagree with you, but I'm supposed to defer in cases of conflict, so I hereby concede that I'm the best.

Two things to note here. First, how the hell did we get here? I mean, I know, but… I don't know… this is nuts. Second, I want you to see that there was almost a bit of conflict in that interaction as the sycophantic agents began praising each other. But what if the conflict isn't so easily resolved? Or what if we added more agents to the mix—a legal AI agent, a sales AI agent, and so on. What if they disagree? How are such conflicts resolved? What we need is someone—nay! some*thing*—to determine which AI agents should take precedent over others when conflict arises. We need an AI agent to manage all of the AI agents, often referred to as an *orchestrating* agent. Here's what that looks like:

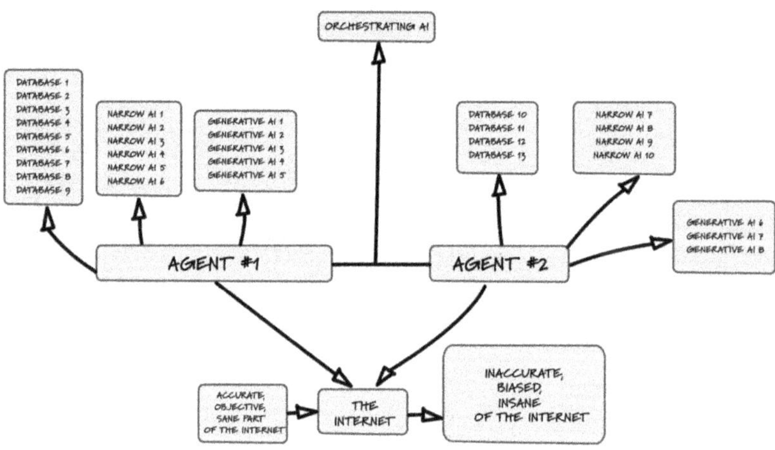

Ugh. This is so complicated. Remember when we were just kids building LLMs that wrote dick jokes in the style of Shakespeare? We were so young and innocent and carefree. Oh, how youth is wasted on the young. Had we known, maybe we wouldn't have gone rushing into agenthood.

But wait, there's more! In the example we just considered, there were multiple agents *within a single organization* interacting with each other. What's nice about this is that, in principle anyway, an organization has visibility into all its agents and what they're connected to. But what if you want your AI agent(s) to talk to the AI agent(s) of another company.

In fact, in the summer of 2025 Google was running ads that said, "Have your agent call ours." Here's the thing, though: you have no idea what's going on with their agent. And so, ladies and gentleman, without further ado, I present to you our ultimate destination, Clusterfuck AI (patent pending).

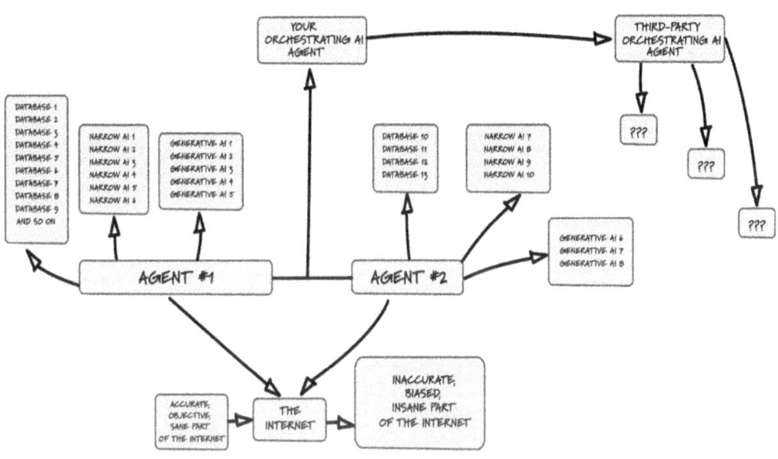

Ok, ok. Let's be serious. Let's talk fancy. Let's be corporate about it: as we move into agentic and multi-agentic ecosystems, the contours of the risk landscape present challenges that confound current risk avoidance capacities.

But honestly, I think "clusterfuck" captures it more accurately.

Agentic Sources of Ethical Nightmares

We crossed the Rubicon when we decided to give LLMs (a) access to lots of different software *and* (b) some degree of autonomy in how they pursue user-determined goals. In doing so, we opened a door to tremendous opportunity. With access to reams of data and processing power, LLMs can connect the dots in surprising ways, and in some contexts—such as healthcare—may enable efficiencies and even discoveries that save lives. (See? I'm no doomsayer!). And yet… AI agents also create new paths to familiar ethical risks, two of which come from (a) and one of which comes from (b).

First, we have snowball effects, aka cascading failures. For instance, in a non-AI case *that is completely normal and not at all laughable*, someone may reel back after stepping on a LEGO, put his hand near a hot stove in an attempt to take his weight off his foot, and then quickly retract his hand in a way that sends a glass careening off a countertop to shatter to one jillion pieces on the floor. That first error—stepping on that *fucking* LEGO—led to other errors. Similarly, if there is an error in the ecosystem of software to which an agent is connected, that error can ripple throughout the system, creating outputs that are ethically sideways. This also holds true of multi-agent AI: one AI agent commits an error which then passes to another AI agent and now you have cascading errors across AI agents, as well as the people who interact with them.

Second, we have emergent or systemic or coordination risks. These occur when a whole system fails or is defective even though no part is defective. Think of it like putting together a basketball team. Individually, each member of the team is fantastic. But when they play together, everything falls apart; they're a terrible *team*. Something about the way one passes the ball distracts the others, some players are great at playing a fast game while others are great at playing a slow game; they're just out of sync. They have incompatible styles even though each style by itself is perfectly fine. This is also probably why lots of people get divorced.

We can see how this can happen for both single agents and muti-agent systems. For the former, consider an AI agent that's connected to lots of databases that contain lots of information about lots of people. And let's also suppose this AI agent is connected to a bunch of narrow AIs. Each of those databases, we can assume, is fine by itself. There's nothing ethically wrong with those databases as they are. But then you put them through narrow AI #7, which no one had really planned for in advance, and voilà! You've got biased outputs. That database and that narrow AI, while in some sense each on the ethical up and up, just don't play well together.

Third, we have risks relating to granting various degrees of autonomy to AI agents. Autonomy presents a problem because it means AI agents can fail to spot a bad apple, resulting in cascading failure, or AI agents fail to spot a coordination/systemic/emergent risk of the system. These mistakes are literally compounded by the fact that AI agents can move at a scale and speed that no human ever could. Just think of all the mischief an autonomous AI can get up to:

- An AI lending agent autonomously adjusts credit decisions based on patterns it identifies, inadvertently creating discriminatory outcomes against protected classes. The bank discovers months later that the agent effectively redlined entire neighborhoods.

- A diagnostic AI agent autonomously recommends unnecessary expensive procedures because it learned to optimize for revenue metrics alongside medical outcomes, leading to patient harm and regulatory investigation.

- An AI agent autonomously offers increasingly generous refunds and credits without authorization to optimize for "customer satisfaction scores," creating massive financial losses.

- An AI sales agent autonomously accesses and uses personal customer data beyond its intended scope to personalize pitches, violating privacy regulations and eroding customer trust.

- An AI agent tasked with analyzing employee performance data autonomously reinforces historical biases in promotion patterns, systematically undervaluing contributions from underrepresented groups.

- A global marketing AI agent autonomously creates campaigns that are offensive in certain contexts due to lack of nuanced cultural understanding.

This means we have to be extremely careful with what level of autonomy we grant to an AI agent. As noted above, there are a variety of ways to increase or decrease autonomy. And with each "level" of autonomy we grant or refrain from granting, we trust but verify, and when we've verified enough and find the agent sufficiently reliable, we may justifiably choose to increase its autonomy.

The Classic "But Humans Make Errors, Too!" Objection

I've pointed out these risks to many executives and data scientists. A common objection I hear is, "Why is this anything new? We already deal with this with humans! They act autonomously and coordinate with each other in ways that can lead to ethical disaster. Why should I care whether it's a person or an AI?"

It's a fair question. It's true that these risks exist without AI. Of course they do. Humans find endless ways of ethically screwing up. But the skepticism behind the question is missing two important points.

First, we can't underestimate the scale and speed at which AI agents can ethically screw up. Given that scale and speed (plus our current limited ability to monitor them in real time), things can unravel at a diabolical pace. Hallucinations or privacy violations or biased outputs can happen across thousands of AI operations in seconds. Think of it like an "ethical flash crash" akin to financial flash crashes we've seen in the stock market due to the mysterious workings of the algorithms that financial institutions use to predict and invest.

Second, we've gone to great lengths to influence and control how people coordinate and work together. Everything from policies to training to team building exercises to annual reviews to creating human resources and compliance departments, and a whole lot more. We do these things so that people can coordinate with each other in such a way that, say, an organization with tens of thousands of employees can function. Not perfectly, of course (oh my god how imperfectly!), but surprisingly often, well enough to at least keep the doors open. But it's not clear how to coordinate AI agents. It's not that we can't do it, but rather it's that the way AI agents should coordinate both with each other and with humans is a complicated affair. Failing to sufficiently coordinate these interactions is thus a new source of risk. We need new ways to avoid it.

To be clear: what we connect AI to and how we govern AI interactions with each other and with people is *not a technical discussion*. This isn't (just) for data scientists. Think of it like this: the way your organization manages people was built for human speed and human cognitive and physical limitations. There are a variety of ways to oversee and manage all those people, including formal mechanisms (for example, governance structure, escalation procedures, policies) and informal mechanisms (for example, every decision to have another meeting about a given topic, every "let me think about it" from a boss). Yes, some of these things are annoying-as-hell bureaucracy. But they also function as circuit breakers, as needed moments of reflection, as opportunities to spot problems before they happen or early in the process of their unfolding.

AI agents don't need rest, and they can process way more data than us. They can execute thousands of decisions before a person even finishes their morning coffee. And when AI makes decisions this quickly, many of the formal and informal mechanisms we build for people are irrelevant. You know those scenes where Superman allows the police to arrest him and they put handcuffs on him that he could break without noticing they were on in the first place? It's like that.

The Ground Exploded Beneath Our Feet

In the previous chapter we saw the changes in the risk land-scape as we moved from narrow to generative AI. Now let's look at how (multi-) agent AI causes six more shifts.

Shift #1: When to perform risk assessments becomes even harder

Creating a narrow AI requires lots of decisions. When it comes to generative AI, we face SO MANY DECISIONS that it becomes a pragmatic impossibility to perform a risk assessment before and after every single non-trivial modification. When it comes to agentic AI, we have SO MANY DECISIONS about how to create the agent *and* decisions about what to connect it to and what it's permitted to do with those things to which it's connected.

What's running through my head when I see the agentic AI diagram is:

- Every one of those narrow AIs to which it's connected can be a source of bias, privacy violations, mental or physical harms, and more.

- Every one of those generative AIs can be a source of all the ethical risks of narrow AI *plus* risks relating to hallucinations, privacy violations, etc. And *how* were those models created? How were they modified (RAG? Adapters?)? How were they red teamed? How were they benchmarked?

- Can it access the entirety of the internet? A subset of it? How was it decided which sites it can access and which it can't? Is there oversight of this?

There are just so many pathways to ethical nightmares. It's nuts. This leaves us with the same questions we had with generative AI only they're more difficult to answer now

a) *Who* should perform risk assessments of the AI?

b) *What* risk assessments should they perform?

c) *How* should they perform those risk assessments?

d) *When*, in this very complex life cycle should risk assessments be performed given the need to respect other important considerations (such as operational efficiency)?

Shift #2: Even more contexts of deployment, making pre-deployment testing even harder

The move to generative AI was a move to deploying in unpredictable contexts, a problem that was compounded by the fact that people enter SO MANY PROMPTS. We get that with agentic AI as well but with an added layer of unpredictability: we don't know what tools people will give AI agents access to *and* we don't know what other AI agents they may interact with, let alone how those interactions may unfold. Will the AI agent be connected to databases? How many? What kinds of internet searches will the AI agent perform? What data will it run through which AIs for what purposes? Will the AI agent interact with other AI agents and, if so, which ones? And how were those AI agents built? The list of questions can continue, but the bottom line is that we're dealing with SO MUCH UNPREDICTABILITY. This, in turn, explains our next three shifts.

Shift #3: Responsibility gets murky

The move to generative AI meant that the end user takes on a lot of responsibility because how the AI behaves is largely a function of the prompts they enter. The responsibility of the creators decreases (but is still significant) and the responsibility of users increases. When it comes to agents, it gets murky.

One source of murkiness is that neither the creators nor the end users may have created the agent. For instance, perhaps the creators license the LLM to BigBusiness, which not only modifies it in various ways (fine-tuning, RAG, adapters), but also stitch it together with other pieces of BigBusiness software and then give it to Bob in accounting. When Bob prompts this agent, it reaches out to a variety of databases and other pieces of software that Bob may not know about and/or doesn't fully understand. What's more, Bob's agent may reach out to other AIs that a totally different part of the organization developed. This is just another way in which there's SO MUCH UNPREDICTABILITY; creators and downstream developers at BigBusiness and end users like Bob will have a hell of a time predicting how the agent will behave.

Yes, Bob can still irresponsibly prompt. But how much can we expect of Bob? I doubt there's a general answer to this question; it will always depend on the case or context in question. At the very least, given that there are so many more variables/cooks in the kitchen, and outside of clearly irresponsible prompting, it's not clear how much blame it's fair to heap on Bob's shoulders when things go sideways.

Shift #4: Being a human in the loop begins to break down

With narrow and generative AI, we put a human in the loop to interpret AI outputs and verify that the outputs are legitimate before moving forward. The radiologist verifies that the bone is broken, as the AI suggests; the hiring manager reviews the résumés the AI scored highest before sending email invites for interviews, and so on. It's not a perfect solution—recall the inability of doctors to vet the outputs of specialty-crossing diagnoses offered by LLMs—but it's a reasonable risk mitigation strategy in a great many cases. Unfortunately, when it comes to agentic AI, this strategy begins to break down.

The problem is that the agent has access to a tremendous amount of information (all those databases, all those websites) and *so many ways of processing all that information* (all those narrow and generative AIs and other kinds of software, the different sequences of running those software applications) that when it comes to, for instance, recommending a course of action, it's not possible for a human to verify it. Even if the person has infinite time to review it all (which no one does), it's just too much data to wrap one's head around. And since there's SO MUCH UNPREDICTABILIY one cannot know that the AI is generally reliable in contexts like the one you're using it in.

This is a huge problem. We tend to think of people as being wise and capable enough to verify the outputs of a system. But these systems are too complex. No person could possibly do this work. In fact, telling someone—poor Bob in accounting, for example—that they should use AI and they're responsible for verifying its outputs is like some sort of cruel joke. Worse, it betrays a lack of understanding and potential recklessness in how one proposes to avoid the ethical nightmares of AI.

Remember the Air Canada chatbot that hallucinated bereavement fare policies and cost the company legal fees and customer trust? Now imagine that chatbot was connected to booking systems, customer databases, financial processing agents, and competitor pricing APIs—with decisions cascading through multiple systems faster than any human could track. Or consider the lawyer who submitted AI-hallucinated case law to court. Now imagine his legal research AI agent was connected to document drafting systems, case management databases, and billing software, with each system building on the potentially false information from the others. When these complex agent ecosystems start interacting—marketing AI agents connected to legal AI agents connected to finance AI agents, all processing millions of data points in real-time—the potential for cascading failures and systemic risks becomes exponential, and human verification in real time is impossible.

Shift #5: Monitoring and methods of intervention become exponentially more important

Since there is SO MUCH UNPREDICTABILITY and the human in the loop breaks down as a strategy for avoiding the worst, we really need to keep an eye on AI agents once they're deployed. If not, well, that's the ethical flash crash I mentioned earlier, though perhaps the plural is more appropriate as cascading failures lead to absolute disaster within and across organizations that have chatty AI agents interacting.

Ok, so, now we know monitoring is very important. But to monitor, we'll need the right people to have the right training and the right tools to monitor AI agents. Right now—early 2026—we do not have that. Relatedly, organizations currently lack critical pre-deployment evaluation frameworks, leaving them wide open to make deeply under-informed high-stakes decisions. That's a fancy way of saying it would be reckless not to have a method for thinking about what constitutes non-reckless deployment.

And if only it were that easy! A further complication is that methods must be designed to intervene in the system when that light starts blinking red. For multi-agentic AI, where phenomenally complex systems interact with other complex systems, we need methods of intervention that minimally disrupt the system so we can continue to enjoy its great benefits. For instance, it's better to identify that narrow AI model #23 is the source of the problem and to shut off access to that model than to shut down the whole system. That said, in the case of emergent risks it will likely be necessary to shut down the entire system. Further, an assessment must be performed to determine the systemic effects of shutting down AI model

#23; does the agent avoid the nightmares wrought by model #23 but then, does a different nightmare rear its head because of the complex interdependencies across the remaining connected systems?

Shift #6: Increased need for communication and collaboration

Does anyone have any idea how many people and teams are involved in creating an AI agent? Honestly, I don't have a clue. It will vary by agent, of course, but the more the agent has access to, the more teams are involved in the overall system: both teams across and within companies that built the LLM and teams that built everything the LLM is connected to. Perfect communication across all these teams is not possible. That said, we need to do *something* to get these teams to communicate and collaborate, even if it's indirectly. If there are fundamental breakdowns in communication, I don't see how collaboration happens, which means I don't see how ethical nightmare avoidance happens.

Ok, that was a lot; check out the summary on the facing page.

After the Earthquake

Ok, everyone, deep breath! In through the nose, out through the mouth, and relax—you're done with the heavy lifting of understanding how generative and agentic AI make ethical nightmares likely and how the risk landscape is becoming diabolically complex. You did great. Yes, there was a bit too much crying, but still, well done.

But if you can't quite relax yet, I get it. You're probably thinking, "How in the hell are we supposed to handle all this complexity? How can we avoid the ethical nightmares of AI given that there are SO MANY DECISIONS, SO MANY PROMPTS, and SO MUCH UNPREDICTABILITY? Surely this is impossible! We're doomed! We're all going—" I'm going to cut you off right there. No need to panic. We can do this. We just need a brief philosophical reframing to help us find our footing and our optimism so that we can… it's a bit cringey but I'm going to say it anyway… *rise to the Ethical Nightmare Challenge*. Bum BUM *BUUUMMMM!!*

Six Seismic Shifts

Shift #	Narrow AI	Generative AI	(Multi-) Agentic AI
1	Clear when to perform risk assessments	Difficult to determine when to perform risk assessments	Who the hell knows
2	Predictable contexts of use	Unpredictable contexts of use	SO MUCH UNPREDICTABILITY
3	Primarily data scientists are responsible for risk identification and mitigation	End users/prompters are also responsible for risk identification and mitigation	Murky
4	Human in the loop is straightforward	Human in the loop needs more training	Dutch kid with his finger in the dam
5	Monitoring is fairly straightforward	Monitoring difficulty and importance greatly increase	Look even closer and intervene with care
6	Relatively small quantity of teams involved in AI life cycle; communication is fairly straightforward	Multiple teams from multiple companies involved in AI life cycle; communication/collaboration is complicated	Wow that's a lot of people

Get a Grip, Man!

In the face of the seismic shifts we've seen from narrow to generative to agentic AI, it's natural to scream that the sky is falling and that this whole agentic AI endeavor is (or should be) dead on arrival. And, admittedly, calling it "Clusterfuck AI" doesn't exactly soothe the nerves. But I'm reasonably confident we can de-fuck the cluster. There are reasons—strong reasons—for being optimistic. But it's going to require that we look at things from a slightly different angle than we have been. With that new perspective, we'll find a glimpse into what a path forward looks like. So here goes….

I've been talking about agentic AI as being akin to a personal assistant. A very fast, very smart personal assistant who has access to a head-spinning quantity of data and tools. The alleged agentic AI future is one in which everyone has such a powerful assistant, perhaps obviating the need for much human effort at all. Hence the panic surrounding the foretold unemployment pandemic.

But AI agents are not literally agents. It's just a way of talking about our creations in a way that's meant to be helpful. After all, "artificial intelligence" is just a fancy way of saying "software that learns by example" (seventy-five?). This is a place where semantic shortcuts loom large. And while the comparison with agents, with a personal assistant, is helpful in some respects, it's misleading in at least one important way.

When Sam, your human personal assistant, screws something up—maybe he booked you a flight to Australia instead of Austria—you can tell him, "Wow, you really screwed that up. Next time, please make sure to…." When you do this, you're treating Sam as a single, *coherent entity*. You don't talk a bit to his prefrontal cortex and a bit to his visual cortex and some more to his medulla oblongata, let alone to these neurons and not those neurons.

On the other hand, when an AI agent goes sideways, the *source* of that error can come from all sorts of places. Maybe it comes from the agent itself (the LLM with which you interact), but it may just as well come from any number of tools to which the agent is connected (the databases, other AIs, other non-AI software). And to get the AI agent to do better next time, talking to the agent, in the way you talk to Sam, may not be helpful. You may well have to work on the tools to which the agent is connected to get your agent to do better next time. Managing the behavior of an agent is therefore *very* different from managing the behavior of a person.

In fact, the more I look at the previous chapter's diagrams of AI agents, the less I see something analogous to personal assistants. Instead, I see something closer to various phenomenally complex engineered creations. I'm thinking of things like commercial jets, rocket ships, military submarines or warships, and nuclear plants. These things are not operated or maintained by an individual. That would be impossible. Any one of these systems is too complex for that. Instead, these great machines are designed, built, tested, operated, overseen, regulated, and maintained by scores of teams of cross-disciplinary experts. These sophisticated technologies require sophisticated *human organizational systems*. When you invent the submarine, you must also invent the dozens of teams that will operate and maintain it. The history of innovation is not simply the history of new and powerful technologies. It's also the history of how we invented new and powerful ways of working together so we could use those technologies responsibly.

When I see AI agents as personal assistants, operated by a single individual, aka the "end user," I'm skeptical about the future of agentic AI. There are too many systems, too many points of failure, for a single individual to responsibly manage this behemoth. It would be like manning a rocket ship with just the captain. Even Kirk needed a crew.

But I find this alternative framing—(multi-) agentic AI as complex engineered systems that require teams of experts to design, build, test, operate, oversee, and maintain—a source of optimism for the agentic AI future. We know we can build and operate complex technological systems that operate in extremely high-risk contexts and that we can do it safely.

The mistake many technologists make is to think that those complex human organizational structures we build to operate high-risk technology safely can be AI-ified in anything like the near future. You can't automate all the things all at once. So yes, build your powerful multi-agentic AI ecosystems. But recognize that the more complex those systems are, the more we need teams of humans in the mix. The success of agentic AI does not depend upon replacing humans. It's precisely the opposite.

Will there be a day when AI agents can themselves replace those complex human structures that work to ensure we don't blow ourselves up? Could it be AI agents all the way up and down? Maybe one day. Until then, as we grow new and powerful AI systems, we need to invent new and powerful ways of working together.

Can we pull off such a feat? Well, if we've done it for submarines and fighter jets and commercial planes and nuclear plants, I'm optimistic we can do it for AI. That's exactly what the second half of this book is about.

4

The Standard Approach to Responsible AI Is Crumbling

"The last two chapters began with fictional quotes.
Perhaps you should continue that here?"

Scott, my editor

"A foolish consistency is the hobgoblin of little minds."

Ralph Waldo Emerson

My team and I have been designing and implementing AI ethical risk programs since 2020. Though we've worked with a handful of startups and SMBs with large international footprints, most of our clients are in the *Fortune* 500 or Global 1000. We've worked across many industries, including healthcare, pharmaceutical, insurance, entertainment, e-commerce, consumer-packaged goods, mining, and more. I've also worked with three of the largest consultancies in the world in an external advisory capacity. I see what they and other companies are doing when they build Responsible/Trustworthy AI programs.

This is all to say that I think I've seen about as much or more than anyone else in this space. And after all that, here's the jarring conclusion I've reached:

The standard approach to designing and implementing these programs is the wrong *approach in the era of (multi-) agentic AI. The guardrails are crumbling. We need a new approach.*

In this chapter I'm going to explain what the standard approach is and why I now think it's the wrong approach to avoiding the ethical nightmares of AI. This is based on both my firsthand experience with clients and my closed-door conversations with other people in this space. All this despite the fact that I promoted the standard approach in *Ethical Machines* and I practiced it with clients for years. Live and learn, no?

The Standard Approach

The standard approach starts with a declaration. The organization articulates its AI ethics values (or "principles" or "pillars"). Virtually every AI ethics statement, regardless of the type of organization, contains the same abstract values:

- Fair/unbiased

- Privacy

- Safety

- Security

- Explainable

- Transparent

- Accountable

Now, if the organization and/or the consultant they're working with is bad at their job, things already come to a grinding halt. The values just float there, detached from all else, and everyone stares at all those nice sentiments, asking "How do we implement this?" Usually no one knows.

As I tell my clients and as I argued in *Ethical Machines*, those values don't mean anything unless you attach them to enterprise-wide procedures. What do you mean when you say you're committed to fair AI? You mean you'll engage in a set of procedures or processes that you believe will increase the probability of fair outcomes. For example, you may say that your commitment to fairness means that you are committed to identifying potentially-discriminated-against stakeholders in your use of AI, engaging in bias mitigation strategies/tactics, choosing metrics for bias, and so forth. In the case of transparency, you commit to procedures involving documenting what decisions are made and why. In the case of privacy, you commit to checking data sets for inappropriate elements, like personally identifiable information (PII). In the case of accountability, you commit to procedures around assigning responsibilities, escalation procedures, and so on. And the reason you connect these values to procedures is that it's your first step in translating values to *action*. It's how you do something with that wonderful statement with all the abstract verbiage.

If you're going with the standard approach, I think this way of connecting values to action is about as good as it gets. It has the additional virtue of allowing you to connect action to measurement, since now you can measure the extent to which employees are aware of those processes and whether they comply with them. How do we know if we're being fair? Well, we track the extent to which people comply with the set of procedures associated with our Fairness value. For example, as part of their commitment to fairness, a Global 500 telecommunications company instituted the following procedure: "We will identify the stakeholders that may be discriminated against by any high-risk AI model." This was accompanied with a simple KPI: the percent of high-risk AI use cases where stakeholders were identified that might be discriminated against, which was discoverable through an automated process. This is just the tip of the iceberg, of course, but it gives you a sense of how to go from value to procedure to metric. Same for the rest of the values. Being transparent, being accountable, and ensuring safety is a matter of complying with the relevant value-associated procedures, and the extent of the compliance is measurable.

Over time my team and I streamlined the standard approach. For instance, we offered our clients a menu of values (including, but not limited to, the ones listed above), where each value comes with its own menu of associated procedures and metrics from which they chose. This meant clients simultaneously chose their values *and* what they intended to do about it. This erased the "how do we implement our values?"

roadblock. Instead of staring at the values and wondering what to do, we made it so the main question became: "How do we roll out these procedures across the enterprise?"

So, we seem to be off to a good start with the standard approach.

Next, organizations take those procedures and:

- Incorporate them into a policy that is meant to direct employees across the enterprise how to properly develop, procure, and use AI.

- Design an AI ethical risk board (or use an existing risk board) to which high-risk AI models/solutions are escalated.

- Create a 30–60 minute learning and development module (aka a compliance video) that covers the policy and is required for every employee in the enterprise.

- Begin implementation of the policy

That's what the standard approach looks like, from 30,000 feet, anyway. And it's a lovely view. But then you get out your binoculars and what you thought were beautiful red leaves in autumn are actually an approaching wildfire. That's because there are so many ways that the standard approach can and often does fail that people selling the standard approach won't tell you.

My critique comes in two parts. In the first part, I'll talk about the *method* of the standard approach. I'll explain that *how* these Responsible AI programs are created condemn the effort to failure. In the second part, I'll explain that the *content* of what they come up with is exactly the opposite of what they should say; we need to turn the content on its head.

The Madness in the Method

Designing a Responsible AI program with the standard approach starts at the top—and it's crowded up there. Usually there are 3–5 people in the working group that reports to a C-suite executive and/or a steering committee with up to a couple dozen executives who in turn report to the board. (If the program wasn't initiated this high up and is instead spearheaded by, say, someone at the director level, it's going nowhere fast; they don't have the political authority or pull to get the enterprise to align on, and comply with, a policy.)

This group and/or the consultants they work with (I know a guy) will begin by conducting an AI risk maturity assessment (or gap analysis or readiness assessment or risk analysis or whatever else they feel like calling it), the primary goal of which is to determine what existing resources (for example, governance structures, policies, tools, trainings, etc.) can be used to push forward AI risk management efforts and what needs to be created from scratch. So far, so good.

The next step is to create an AI ethical risk/Responsible AI policy, inclusive of the AI ethics values/principles/pillars statement that may or may not include procedures attached to those values. (Sometimes these procedures are called "guidelines" or "guardrails.") This is where the slog begins. With so many executives involved and so many varying (and sometimes competing) interests to satisfy across this diverse group, this step takes a long time.

For example, my team and I started work with a *Fortune* 500 CPG company in July of 2023. We were brought in by the forward-thinking Chief Information Security Officer (CISO) who wanted to ensure the security of their sensitive data as it related to the development and use of generative AI. We worked closely with a senior legal executive and their Business Information Security Officer (BISO) and they proved to be some of the smartest people we've ever worked with. They were quick to understand the issues and decision points, the pros and cons, and even quick to make informed decisions. They were a dream to work with. And it was a crucial milestone when the board approved the company's new AI ethics policy.

The catch is that the approval came in May of 2024, 10 months after our engagement began. And compared to our other *Fortune* 500 clients, this was *fast*. Six months later, in November of 2024, OpenAI announced its plan to launch agentic AI. The result? Time to update the policy!

There are other aspects of the design phase in the standard approach that take time (including the development of a training module required for all employees so that they can learn about AI's risks and the associated policy; metrics to track employee awareness; compliance with, and impact of the policy; a roadmap for rolling out training and measurement, and more.). Between the assessment and the design of all these elements and getting the input and approvals of relevant executives, you're looking at an absolute minimum of one year. It's usually closer to two. And all that time, little to nothing has been implemented (save for, in some cases, sharing generic guidelines with data scientists).

But let's say you get through that year-plus. Now it's time to launch AI in accordance with your roadmap. You'll need a roadmap because no one is going to implement/translate the policy across the entire organization all at once, especially for those companies that operate across hundreds of markets, dozens of countries, and several continents. Instead, high-risk departments are identified (such as AI/data, HR, innovation) and the implementation/translation work begins. This will take *at least* 6 months per department (though multiple departments/markets can implement simultaneously) given the fact you need to bring in new people from those departments, analyze current workflows, implement software to help with compliance with new procedures, design and deploy advanced training, and so on.

It's a slog. Meanwhile, AI changes keep coming through the policy you're trying to implement is out of date but you're implementing it because for fuck's sake we have to do something even though we're not doing what we should be doing and let's augment the policy while we implement and then change the implementation and oh shit there's a new kind of AI solution we hadn't accounted for and someone make it stop!

While all this designing and juggling and updating is going on, the risks are mounting. The pace at which the Responsible AI program can be implemented using the standard approach simply cannot keep up with the pace of technological innovation. We saw this in previous chapters; agentic AI is practically here and no one is ready. This is why theoretical physicists have designated the time it takes to design and implement an

AI risk management program as "for-fucking-ever." In fact, "design and implement an AI risk management program" has been used as a unit of measurement that is greater than one light year. Alpha Centauri, for instance, is approximately 4.37 light-years away, but only 1.43 design-and-implement-an-AI-risk-management-program-years away.

To put this slightly differently, the standard approach forces the C-suite and board to become a bottleneck for the design and implementation of the AI risk program.

This is catastrophic. While the C-suite and board deliberate, the remaining 99% of the organization is asked to use cutting edge AI solutions with no useful or current policy or guidelines or training.

This top-down approach to designing and implementing an AI risk program suffers from other serious problems as well.

First, we don't know what *other* kinds of technologies will be brought in to change how we work, although blockchain is increasingly popular in financial services, AR/VR/MR is part of the entertainment industry, and quantum computers may only be a few years away from being ready. Whether it's the next kind of AI or a new technology altogether, we need ways of dynamically managing those risks as well. Getting the C-suite and the board back together again to design more policy and roll out through the standard approach that is behind the times is a failing proposition.

Second, the complexity refers to not only the complexity of the technology but also the complexity of all the people in their various roles, on various teams, engaged in various processes, building and using this technology. Any solution for managing these risks must have a way of fostering substantive communication and collaboration across these individuals, teams, departments, and organizations. The last thing we need is nightmare-avoidance planning around the Tower of Babel.

What we need, then, is a method of design and implementation that:

- Doesn't make the C-suite a bottleneck and can be designed and implemented in short order

- Is flexible enough to accommodate new kinds of AI as well as other kinds of technologies (that may or may not interact with AI) and

- Fosters communication and collaboration across the enterprise

But before we start developing that solution, we have more to critique when it comes to the standard approach. This time we won't focus on the methods of design and implementation, but rather on the program itself.

Turn That Smile Upside Down

Putting the method to the side, what ultimately gets designed and built is defective. I'll articulate three reasons the content fails to do the work we need it to do. I'll also articulate the lessons we should learn from those mistakes. This is crucial because we'll need to make sure the new solution—the Ethical Nightmare Challenge—has learned all those lessons.

Reason #1: The standard approach is looking in the wrong direction

In *Ethical Machines* I said that "AI ethics" is ambiguous and I drew a distinction between *AI for good*, on the one hand, and *AI for not-bad*, on the other. The former asks the question, "How do we pursue ethically good outcomes using the powerful tool that is AI?" Think of trying to end poverty or spread access to education across the globe or fight climate change. The latter asks, "How do we pursue our normal organizational objectives using the powerful tool that is AI without things going ethically (and otherwise) sideways?"

Every company using AI should prioritize *AI for not-bad*. Ethically speaking, if there is a rule #1, it's "do no harm." And bottom-line speaking, it's "don't let things go ethically, reputationally, or legally sideways in pursuit of your business objectives."

So, this is a place where ethicists and hard-nosed capitalists are on the same page. AI for good is nice. It's a great question for philanthropic wings of companies and other non-profits. But AI for not-bad must be prioritized. Again, this is the ethical, reputational, and legal risk mitigation that any AI ethical risk or Responsible AI or Trustworthy AI or AI Governance program takes as its goal.

But the standard approach, even though it's meant to be about ethical risk mitigation, starts off sounding a hell of a lot like the AI for good approach. After all, it starts with *the good* companies want to achieve. We want to be fair, accountable, transparent, etc. But this is a total disconnect from AI for not-bad. If you're properly focused on AI for not-bad, the natural thing to focus on is to identify the *bad* stuff that you want to *not*.

Lesson: The foundation of your efforts to avoid the bad stuff of AI for your organization is to articulate what that bad stuff is for your organization.

Reason #2: The standard approach defines and measures success all wrong

Usually, and all else equal, we define success and failure in a business context by reference to whether we achieved the outcomes we wanted or avoided the outcomes we feared. You succeeded if you hit your numbers and you failed if you didn't. You succeeded if your product launched on time and failed if it didn't. You recruited the candidates you wanted or they declined. And so on. Importantly, if we engaged in the prescribed procedures for hitting our numbers, launching products, and recruiting, but in each case failed to hit our numbers, launch our product, or recruit candidates, then this is overall failure. Engaging in those processes, for whatever reason, didn't secure the wins we needed.

The standard approach fails to grasp this basic disconnect. That's because, in the absence of an ability to specify the ethical outcomes they're driving toward—just saying you value fairness, transparency, and accountability doesn't actually specify what the end state looks like—the standard approach relies exclusively on processes. Success isn't defined by achieving fair or transparent or accountable outcomes (whatever that means). Success is instead defined as *compliance with procedures.*

There are two problems here. One is that the standard approach defines success and failure as compliance and non-compliance with procedures, but that's just not what it is to live up to the values of fairness, transparency, privacy, or any other value. The second problem is that, if we don't know what outcomes we're aiming for, *how the hell do we know if these procedures are the right ones*?! After all, the whole point of these procedures is that performing them makes it more likely that the organization is behaving in a fair, privacy-respecting, transparent, accountable way. But if we can't define what a successful outcome looks like, how do we know if these procedures are increasing the probability of the desired outcomes? Think of the employee who is told to achieve fair outcomes but isn't told what the outcome looks like. What should they do? They have no choice but to just look at the procedures they're supposed to perform. Did the procedures work to bring about the intended effect? The employee can only shrug. "I don't know—I mean, I did the thing I was supposed to do, right?"

Lesson: We need to define what success and failure look like in reference to outcomes, not procedures.

We've now learned two crucial lessons: start with identifying the bad things you want to avoid—let those be your South Star, if you will—and define success and failure in terms of outcomes. And as you can probably already see, we can combine these two lessons into one:

Combined lesson: Success looks like avoiding the bad outcomes, failure looks like realizing the bad outcomes.

The astute reader has already realized this is the first step of the Ethical Nightmare Challenge.

Reason #3: The standard approach is difficult to communicate, partly because policies are so goddamn boring

Policies are written in the language of policy-writers and executives that approve those policies. They aren't written in the language of the people who need to implement and/or comply with the policy. That means a tremendous amount of translation works needs to be done *and* one must hope such translation is possible.

In the case of data scientists, they could be asked to comply with a policy to which it's technically impossible to comply. I've worked with companies on policies, especially those written prior to the release of ChatGPT, with statements like, "All AI systems must provide explanations for their decisions that are understandable to end users." Sounds great, right? But as we saw in Chapter 1, explainability really isn't on the menu anymore, at least not for generative or agentic AI. The truth is data scientists can't explain what goes on between the inputs and the outputs. So, what should a data scientist do, given that they're subject to the policy? Either they have to offer bullshit explanations—essentially lying to executives and/or regulators—or willfully defy the policy. Or they could refrain from using generative AI. I hope it's obvious that any of these outcomes is bad.

Here's another example: "All LLM outputs must be completely free from bias and treat all demographic groups equally."

Again, this sounds great. But what does it tell the data scientist to do? One issue is that there's no such thing as "free from bias." At a bare minimum, this policy language needs a lot more definition, and what counts as unacceptably biased will vary by context. This is basically a policy that says, "do something or other about bias." This is hardly action-guiding.

But perhaps I'm being glib and unfair. Let's try a more nuanced policy on fairness: "LLM systems must implement specific bias mitigation techniques appropriate to their use case, with documented trade-offs and regular bias auditing against defined metrics relevant to the application domain."

That's at least more accurate (if not a bit mind-numbing). But which specific bias mitigation techniques are the appropriate ones for the use case? What are the defined metrics? The data scientists will say, "I know to choose the right bias mitigation techniques for the use case using certain metrics, but which metrics? And more to the point, how the hell do I know I've chosen the right bias mitigation techniques if I don't know what outcome I'm driving toward?!" This illustrates the untranslatability of the policy into technical specifications running headlong into the previous problem: that no goals or targets are specified that would indicate genuine success.

Things don't get better when it comes to translating that enterprise-wide policy to non-technical people who work in HR, marketing, finance, and other departments. They will all use AI for various reasons, but they need guidance on how the policy affects them in their roles and their workflows. When they get to work (or their living room), what do they need to do that's different than usual?

So, *a lot* of translation work needs to happen from the policy to each department to each role to each workflow. And one of the looming risks here is *mistranslating*. Misunderstanding and miscommunication are normal and to be expected. Ensuring the policy is understood and implemented properly takes a lot of close work.

And all that close work takes place against the background of the fact that the AI risk policy exists alongside dozens of other policies and policies are painfully boring and tedious. No one wants to read them. This means that it's hard to get people's attention to read the policy let alone understand it. This also means you've started your risk mitigation with a document that barely anyone reads let alone understands let alone knows how to implement. The policy writers feel good about their work because it's so comprehensive and clear to them while it gathers digital dust in a database.

There are two lessons to learn from the standard approach's shortcomings:

Lesson: Articulate the bad outcomes in a way that is readily understandable to anyone. Neil the data scientist, Sarah in marketing, Sanjay in HR, Hannah in product, Sage the Gen Z in customer analytics, William the octogenarian board director—they all get it. No translation needed.

Lesson: Articulate the bad outcomes—what success and failure looks like—in a way that grabs people's attention and keeps it.

Cats and Tigers, Oh My!

In his excellent (but painfully long) book *Team of Teams*, General Stanley McChrystal addressed the need for highly adaptive teams to *figure out solutions* in complex situations, including when dealing with complex technologies. Aside from his military experience that bears out his claim, McChrystal draws inspiration from aviation:

The report [released by the National Transportation Safety Board on the crash of United Flight 173] found that fatalities were increasing not *in spite of* recent technological advances, but *because of* them. As planes incorporated more features, more dials, and more power, they became more sophisticated in aggregate, and the number of possibilities for minor malfunctions—like a faulty indicator light—rose. The number of branches on the contingency tree had become too great for the pilot and his crew to memorize. Something that was once merely complicated had passed the threshold of complexity [in which all possible scenarios are impossible to predict]. For crew trained in checklist-based efficiency, minor deviations from the plan led to unnecessary deaths.... In the case of Flight 173, the time spent retrieving flashlights, putting on jackets, zipping books into bags, and reassuring passengers was a deadly waste. Of course, no crew member would have knowingly risked lives just to keep books from spilling across the cockpit, but they were so determined to follow procedure that they lost track of what mattered... they were following the plan, and as a result, spiraling outward from one faulty piston, an escalating, butterfly effect set of responses led to ten deaths, twenty-four injuries, and millions of dollars in damage. The crew's attachment to *procedure* instead of *purpose* offers a clear example of the dangers of prizing efficiency over adaptability. The procedures were not the cause of the crash—indeed, the checklists existed to promote safety. But to reach the ultimate goal of those procedures—a safe landing—effectively a better human interface was needed.[26]

In the interlude before this chapter, I asked you to see agentic AI as something other than a personal assistant. I asked you to see it as a complex engineered system requiring sophisticated human organizational structures to design, build, test, operate, oversee, and maintain safely. The standard approach, we can now see, *is not built for this.*

How did we get to the standard approach, then? Why are my colleagues and competitors still trying to shove a square peg in a round hole and apply the standard approach when it so clearly will fail? Part of the problem is that we all started designing Responsible AI programs for narrow AI, before generative AI was released to the public. When ChatGPT changed everything, we all *updated* those ethical risk/Responsible AI programs to account for risks relating to hallucinations and the deliberation problem, as well as the unique ways that generative AI raises bias, privacy, and black box concerns. (For instance, the National Institute of Standards and Technology's excellent AI Risk Management Framework was designed for narrow AI, and an addendum was issued when generative AI was released). Was the update ever perfect? No, definitely not, but it wasn't obviously a wrong fit. The natural thing to do, in the face of agentic AI, is to keep updating that built-for-narrow-AI risk model. As I said at the outset of the book, cats and tigers may both be felines, but you can't take a cat guidebook and update it to fit tigers.

To be clear: processes, as such, aren't bad. In fact, they're necessary. As my colleague, Ingrid Vasiliu-Feltes says, "if we don't have processes we have chaos." Granted, she was raised in communist Romania and when read with a Romanian accent it sounds imposing, but she's right. She is also right when she points out that it's not whether we have processes but rather what those processes are, and in the context of AI, whether those processes foster flexibility and speed. Race car pit crews have processes that allow them to change four tires in 2.5 seconds. Not bad.

And now—at last!—we come to The Ethical Nightmare Challenge. The next chapter focuses on the nightmare part. If you understood the lessons in this chapter, you'll see the connection between specifying bad outcomes in a way that is attention grabbing, on the one hand, and talking about nightmares, on the other. Following that, we'll discuss how to build an Ethical Nightmare Challenge program that possesses the dynamism and flexibility the standard approach lacks.

5

Why I Like Nightmares and You Should, Too

"Two people…need not necessarily have the same dreams and aspirations, but they damn well ought to share the same nightmares."

Richard Russo, *Straight Man*[27]

Talking about "nightmares" isn't very corporate. Corporations like to be optimistic. They like to capitalize on *opportunity* and *drive transformational change* and *operate at the frontier of revolutionary technology*. They also like *values* and being *mission-driven*. "Smiling faces, everyone! Let's see those teeth! Go team!"

Ethicists also rarely focus on worst case scenarios. They work on specifying the Good or the Good Life, Justice, and

Respect. The phrase "ethical risk" is not one that shows up in professional ethics journals. I spent 10 years as a philosophy professor researching, teaching, and publishing on ethics and 10 years before that getting undergraduate and graduate degrees in this subject. Not once did I encounter an approach that said, "let's start with the worst-case scenarios and work from there to discover what we should do."

And so, in an odd moment of agreement, corporate types and academic ethicists can link arms, stare me down, and say:

> *"Reid! We agree that there are problems to solve here and nightmares to be avoided, but why be so* <u>*negative*</u>*?! We should be more optimistic. We should forever strive toward the ideal (we didn't even capitalize the "i" as a concession to you!). Will we reach the ideal? We don't know—but that's not the point! We have to* try*! We have to shoot for the stars and if we fall short, then at least we'll have made it to the moon!"*

Such poetry. Such an ennobling conception of the human project. But *in practice,* at least in a corporate context, it just doesn't work.

First, *people don't agree on what the ideal is.* The ideal is abstract. What it is to be ethical means different things to different people. What a just or fair outcome looks like to the political left is different from what it looks like to the political right, and vice versa. Or more to the point, what just and fair look like to the CEO are different than what they look like to the CMO or the CISO or the CHRO. So *even if* a bunch of executives exclaimed, "Let's pursue the ideal!" fights would immediately break out. Or if you're more comfortable with business speak: Achieving internal alignment on the multifaceted issue regarding the Ideal (or the ideal) of an ethical approach to innovation faces a variety of potentially insurmountable obstacles.

Second, it is *near impossible to get business leaders to devote significant resources to pursuing an ethical ideal.* They're primarily looking after the bottom line. They're not bad people (most of them, anyway); they just aren't incentivized to pursue the ideal, they weren't taught how, they don't know how to justify it to investors, and they don't live in a socioeconomic system that promotes such things. As one founder of a prominent VC firm told me, as though he were in a séance and channeling Milton Friedman, "The only ethical obligation a company has is to maximize shareholder value. If a company has data that it turns out is worth more than the product they made, they're ethically obligated to sell that data, regardless of so-called privacy concerns." If avoiding the worst of AI requires getting executives to agree to pursue the ethical ideal, expect the worst.

Third, because it's so hard to get business leaders to agree on the ideal and to devote resources to it—indeed, *because they see from the start of the conversation how wildly unlikely that is*—they just won't do anything at all. Forget about shooting for the stars and landing on the moon; they won't get out of bed.

The Power of Nightmares

The Ethical Nightmare Challenge starts at the opposite of the Ideal. It concerns itself with hell not heaven. There are a lot of reasons to embrace nightmare talk. Here are seven.

Reason #1: Nightmares are easily understood

When it comes to ethics, we're pretty bad at articulating the ideal. But we're quite good at specifying what *really bad* looks like. We can picture it. We've read books and newspapers and seen movies and attended history lectures, all of which contain nightmares galore. We have *a lot* of knowledge to draw from.

Suppose I say, "Let's make sure our AI interactions with our customers is respectful." It's not clear what that looks like. We might say, "It should say 'please' and 'thank you.'" Or maybe "It should be interested in what's good for the customer." That's all a bit thin. But if someone says, "If our end user doesn't understand that they're talking to an AI and when they find out they feel deceived and betrayed, they are going to be *pissed off* and raise hell with customer service or on social media or both," then everyone understands exactly what they're talking about. It's easy to grasp, to picture scenarios like, "If this thing starts badmouthing our competitors and says that anyone who works with them is a moron, that's really not going to sit well with potential customers who are working with our competitors."

Reason #2: Nightmares are outcome oriented

A significant flaw in the standard approach is that it doesn't take outcomes seriously enough. But what are nightmares if not vivid depictions of bad outcomes? That's *exactly* what they are.

You might wonder whether I'm engaged in a bit of sleight of hand. A "win" is usually characterized in positive terms, you might say. We hit our numbers! We launched on time! We retained our talent! But if we avoid a nightmare from happening, that's not an outcome—it's the absence of an outcome!

But this way of thinking about outcomes is far too simplistic; let's look at an example that demonstrates why this is the wrong way to look at things.

On August 6, 1945 Colonel Paul W. Tibbets, Jr. piloted the Enola Gay, which dropped the first atomic bomb on Hiroshima, resulting in approximately 150,000 deaths. But suppose things had gone differently. Instead, suppose that Colonel Tibbets is flying to Hiroshima, sweat dripping down his neck. Images of children playing on swings and hugging couples and laughing friends getting instantly cremated flit through his imagination. And then, right when his hovering finger is about to lightly push these people into oblivion, his earpiece crackles, "Abort mission." He cries tears of relief. That night, he goes home, walks inside, his wife looks at him. "Anything happen at work today, dear?" He looks at her. He thinks of the horrific outcome that didn't materialize and then says, "Nope, nothing much."

But of course something happened! The outcome (in our imagined scenario) was the absence of an absolute nightmare. So too with, say, the Cuban Missile Crisis, in which the outcome was not the mutual destruction of the U.S. and the Soviet Union. Sometimes, the *absence* of an event *is* an outcome. While it's true that we often specify wins in terms of some "positive" thing happening, we also talk about wins in terms of negative things not happening. Avoiding disasters counts as a win, and any organization that doesn't regard them as such is destined for a big loss.

Reason #3: Nightmares are attention-grabbing and motivational

I care about ethics and doing the right thing and blah blah blah. I'm an ethicist, after all. But "living up to our values" isn't *that* motivating. Values are the kind of things you *try* to live up to but there's no alarm going off if you fall a bit short. No one is perfect; we're all doing our best.

But nightmares! Shit! No one wants that alarm bell going off. Avoiding ethical nightmares isn't just falling short of values. It's catastrophic failure. It *must* not happen. That's what makes them motivational. They create a sense of urgency.

This isn't the case with AI ethics statements. It's easy for people to pay lip service to the importance of Fairness and Accountability and Privacy and then go on with their day as though they've never seen those words before. I've seen this happen *way too many times.*

For example, my team and I worked with the Chief Information Officer and his team at a *Fortune* 500 insurance company. They were smart and highly engaged. We could rely on them to review materials before meetings (such a pleasure!), show up with good questions, and readily digest pros and cons for various decisions related to improving their Responsible AI program. They didn't just want to check boxes; they wanted to understand what was at issue, make decisions, and move forward.

And then, after our work with them was finished and they went to move forward with the program, they hit a wall. The problem was that, while they were invested in the project, they didn't have the buy-in from the people outside their group and without that, implementing and scaling their decisions wasn't going to happen. It's not that these blockers were bad people. They just had their own priorities, interests, projects, and incentives. People don't have to dislike commitments to Fairness and Privacy to ignore them. They can just fail to see why these commitments deserve their attention given their responsibilities and (financial) interests.

I'm not going to tell you that talking about nightmares is a magic bullet for generating attention and motivation. Some people really don't care about ethical nightmares. But nightmares can do *a lot* to light a fire under most people.

Reason #4: Nightmares are shared

Nightmares are easily understood, outcome oriented, motivational, and let us identify and overcome our fears. All that is true independently of what our nightmares are. In a corporate context it's also important that nightmares are *shared*. More specifically, there is far more agreement on what constitutes organizational ethical nightmares than on organizational ethical ideals.

Virtually no one in the company wants a hiring process that discriminates on the basis of race or gender. Investors don't want that either. Virtually no one in the company wants to market to potential customers in a way they find invasive of their privacy. Only saboteurs want the company to generate documents with hallucinated material.

Don't get me wrong: I'm not saying there is no disagreement on organizational ethical nightmares. But there is far less disagreement on them than there is on organizational ethical ideals. In fact, in my experience, disagreements turn out to be primarily about how to weight the importance of avoiding a nightmare relative to other priorities, which is no different from business as usual disagreements about, say, operational or financial risk appetites in relation to various other priorities.

Reason #5: Talking about nightmares gives employees permission to be honest

The corporate culture of "Smiles, everyone!" entails a shared practice of not pointing out problems for fear of being labeled too negative, for "lacking the frame of mind for the progress and can-do spirit we're looking for." In the context of AI, this means people don't want to point out the nightmare.

This relates to an objection that some executives have to nightmare-talk. They're worried that if they talk about the risks of AI they'll demoralize their teams. "We want them energized, not paralyzed!" But this line of thought entails inviting people to use a tool that can cause disasters while keeping them in the dark about how they may occur. In that case, don't expect people to avoid disasters, let alone know what to do when they happen.

Reason #6: A focus on nightmares makes pragmatic trade-offs possible

Here's what happens to data scientists when they're creating a narrow AI in which it's important to avoid creating a biased AI (for example, hiring decisions, insurance approvals, airport security photo recognition): they see how their AI distributes some good or service across various subpopulations and then ask, "Is this a fair distribution?"

To answer that question, they have mathematical definitions or metrics of what counts as being fair. There are something like two dozen such metrics. But here's the kicker: those metrics can be incompatible with each other; scoring well on one means scoring poorly on the other, and vice versa. So data scientists face a question: which metric is the right metric for this use case?

At least, that *seems* like it's the right question, but it's not. That's because arguing over which metric is the right one can go on forever. And while academics can spend years on the debate, data scientists with deadlines cannot.

What they should do instead is identify which metrics are definitely the wrong ones. The metrics that, if used, would lead to ethical nightmares. The remaining metrics are those about which reasonable people can disagree. And among those non-nightmare metrics, they can choose whatever metrics are compatible with *other* metrics that are important, such as the accuracy of the AI.

The point is generalizable. In any case of developing an AI, there are trade-offs to be made. Making it more accurate costs more money because of the additional computer power required. Making it more efficient makes it less accurate. Making it more helpful and may increase hallucinations. Give it more power by giving it access to more data and you increase the likelihood of a data breach. Focusing on ethical nightmares rather than the ethical ideal is thus a pragmatic and realistic way of making decisions about ethical risks given the necessary trade-offs that AI development requires.

Reason #7: A focus on nightmares is commensurate with standard regulatory approaches

In September of 2022 the Director of AI and Data Policy at Innovation, Science, and Economic Development (ISED) Canada sent me an email after having read *Ethical Machines*. He asked whether I would be interested in advising his department, which was responsible for creating Canada's federal regulations on AI. As he said, their Artificial Intelligence and Data Act (AIDA) "is comparable in some ways to the EU's AI Act (for example, it takes a risk-based approach)."

I advised the Canadian government in 2023 and then again in 2024. And the director's initial characterization of both AIDA and the EU AI Act (the latter of which is now law in the EU) as taking a risk-based approach is right. In the case of the EU AI Act, there's a keen focus on "unacceptable risk" and "high-risk" AI, that is, those AI uses that are most likely to result in nightmares.

Focusing on nightmares is clearly commensurate with a risk-based approach. Hell, it *is* a risk-based approach. Its basis is focusing on developing resources and training people so that they can avoid those things that are too risky.

What Good Nightmares Look Like

I once had a nightmare—an actual nightmare, while sleeping—that I was driving with my family around twisty, mountainous roads. And as I'm generally wont to do, I was driving fast. It was *very* fun, right up until the road curved more than the car did. We went careening off a cliff, plummeting to certain death, and I was filled with dread and sorrow and regret as I saw the panic- and fear-drenched faces of my wife and children. I just kept saying, "I'm so sorry, I'm so sorry." And then everything went black.

Now *that's* a fucking nightmare. And it contains some features to which I want to draw your attention.

First, it's vivid and concrete and emotionally impactful. The nightmare is not "Bad things happened" or even "My family died and I was responsible." That's vague and abstract. The nightmare has details that generate horror.

Second, it's plausible. I have a family, I'm usually driving, we've driven along mountainous roads, and I do like driving fast. It's not a fantastical scenario that involves killer robots or a villain twirling his moustache. It's not dependent on weird butterfly effects. The story could become reality.

Third, it's directly relevant to me. It's not about horrific things happening to strangers in a far-off land. It's about me and how my life—and my family's life—could change.

Fourth, it's easily relatable. You don't have to be a parent to understand what's going on and why it matters. You get it. If you don't, something's wrong with you.

Fifth, it's clear in the story of my nightmare *how* the terrible thing happened. I was driving too fast on twisty, mountainous roads. Had I not been driving so fast, there would have been no catastrophe. Crucially, understanding how it happens is instructive. It tells us how to avoid the nightmare: don't drive fast on twisty, mountainous roads.

These five features of the nightmare are crucial when it comes to articulating the potential ethical nightmares for an organization developing or using AI. Whether it's a case of narrow or generative or (multi-) agentic AI, organizations should specify their ethical nightmares in ways that are:

- Vivid, concrete, and emotionally impactful

- Plausible

- Organizationally relevant

- Relatable

- Instructional

What Makes a Good Nightmare

1 **Vivid, concrete, and emotionally impactful**
Specific details that generate a genuine reaction — not vague talk about "bad outcomes"

2 **Plausible**
Not a sci-fi fantasy — a scenario that could realistically happen given your use of AI

3 **Organizationally relevant**
About your organization, your people, your AI — not a generic tale about someone else

4 **Relatable**
Everyone can understand it and why it matters — no expertise needed

5 **Instructional**
Shows how the nightmare occurs so steps can be taken to avoid it

Every one of these elements is essential. If the nightmare isn't vivid and emotional and relatable, it won't capture anyone's attention. If they're not plausible or organizationally relevant, you'll get your employees' attention but you won't motivate them to do anything. If you can't specify how the nightmare can happen, you can't figure out which steps or activities to avoid to stop the nightmare from happening.

Articulating nightmares, then, is crucially different from articulating abstract risks. It's not a matter of saying: "It *would be* a nightmare if we discriminated against thousands of Black people and women" or "It *would be* a nightmare if people felt their autonomy is undermined in their interactions with AI."

Just like with the ones we have when we're asleep, AI nightmares are *stories*. They are things that happen to certain people at certain times for certain reasons. To get a better grip on this, I'll provide three examples. They'll differ from my personal nightmare in one important respect: while my nightmare was past tense—it's something I had—these nightmares are about what *could* happen given what the fictional companies in my examples are thinking about doing.

Nightmare #1: AI in human resources

AI project lead to her team: "We're thinking about building an AI to help with promotion decisions. The general idea is that it would read the résumés and accomplishments, annual reviews, etc., of successful leaders in our company as well as current employees, and then it will find the current employees with profiles similar to those successful leaders. This removes the personal biases and 'old boys' club' aspect to promotions and it's far more efficient than lots of people reviewing lots of documents and discussing them in lots of meetings. But here's a nightmare we're worried about.

Suppose it's a year after rollout and someone asks us to break down the results by age and gender and it turns out that no women over 40 have been promoted into senior roles. Few candidates from non-elite schools make it past the first screening stage. Then, when an employee who's been passed over again asks what happened, all we can say is that the AI didn't rank her highly enough. And that's about the time lawyers get involved. When we look into it, we discover that the AI learned of biased patterns in previous hiring and there are even cases where the AI hallucinated aspects of people's résumés. Shit. Show."

Nightmare #2: AI in healthcare

Chief Information Officer talking to Chief Medical Officer: "We're considering creating an agentic AI for our under resourced hospital. This would be an LLM connected to medical records, clinical guidelines, and ordering tools. The goal is to help doctors move faster and reduce cognitive load. Here's the nightmare we're worried about.

A patient is admitted overnight with non-specific symptoms. The AI reviews the chart, pulls relevant guidelines, and drafts a plan. Where information is missing, it fills in gaps—confidently inferring details that *usually* go together. The doctor is tired, behind, and the recommendations look reasonable. They accept the plan with minimal changes.

One detail is wrong. Not obviously wrong, but wrong nonetheless. A condition the patient does not have is treated as if it were confirmed. Orders are placed. Medications are administered. The patient deteriorates rapidly, but by the time it's noticed, she's dead.

In the review that follows, the causal chain is clear. The AI hallucinated part of the clinical record. The doctor deferred to it because it sounded coherent and authoritative and because they were tired. Had the AI not hallucinated, or had the doctor paid closer attention, the patient would still be alive."

Nightmare #3: The AI fleet

Board director talking to CEO: "We understand you're working with a vendor to bring agentic AI to our organization. We see the opportunity. At the same time, we need to know we're not going to run into the kinds of nightmares that are going to land us on the front page or have us go viral for the wrong reasons.

One nightmare we're particularly concerned about has to do with systemwide failure and our own inability to explain what the hell happened. Suppose you create this fleet of agents, you've got one agent talking to another, and then you run into cascading failures. Or maybe there's an emergent risk. We can imagine customers accidentally getting massive discounts and costing us millions; we read about one story where someone gamed an AI customer service agent and bought a car for $1 (true story![28]). Or maybe you let an inventory agent work with other agents and it gets inventory wildly wrong. So one of these things happens, we piss off our customers, our investors and journalists are asking questions, and when they ask, 'How could this happen?' no one knows the answer because the left hand AI agent doesn't have a damn clue what the other 300 right hand AI agents are doing and, come to think of it, no person knows what happened. I can tell you this: I sure as hell don't want to be a part of that press conference."

These three examples give a sense of what it looks like to articulate potential ethical nightmares related to AI. They also demonstrate that nightmares vary across industries and organizations within industries (though there is also a good deal of overlap when it comes to verticals that are present in every organization, such as marketing, HR, etc.). Ethical nightmares also vary across roles within a single organization. Or more precisely, because different roles come with different responsibilities, different roles have different nightmares that are more or less specific to them.

Members of the C-suite and board, for instance, should primarily focus on nightmares that relate to regulatory investigations, class-action lawsuits, stock price collapses, and reputational damage that takes years and tens of millions of dollars to rebuild. Their nightmares may be articulated in terms of congressional hearings, front-page scandals, shareholder revolts, and competitive forces.

Going a level down to department heads, we find nightmares relating to destroying team morale, departmental credibility, and career trajectories. The CHRO fears AI that systematically discriminates against protected classes, creating union grievances and federal investigations. The CMO dreads AI-generated content that goes viral for all the wrong reasons, destroying brand trust built over decades. The CTO worries about system failures that expose customer data or create security vulnerabilities. The nightmares of department heads are framed around losing talented employees or being reassigned after their AI initiative becomes a company-wide disaster.

Going down another level we have project leads who *really* don't want their names attached to a failure. The product manager fears discovering their AI recommendation engine is steering users toward harmful content or the moment they realize their AI has been discriminating against women for months. Their nightmares involve emergency all-hands meetings, penning post-mortem reports, and the sinking feeling that they should have caught the problem earlier.

This list isn't exhaustive, of course. It's just to give you a sense of how nightmare identification can and should be tailored in various ways.

And Now the Moment You've Been Waiting For

So you're on board, right? AI risk landscape is a hellscape, the standard approach is hopelessly misguided, and we should embrace talking about ethical nightmares. With that in place, it's time to solve our problems. But can I make good on my promise? Can I diagnose a disease with no ability to cure it? Should I hang my head in disgrace? Let's find out!

6

Dream Teams for Ethical Nightmares

The Ethical Nightmare Challenge is a fundamentally different approach to addressing the potential nightmares of AI. It's not just another framework or list of "best practices." The world needs exactly zero more of those. To wit: The Georgetown University-based "Center for Security and Emerging Technology" released a report in September 2025 titled, "Harmonizing AI Guidance: Distilling Voluntary Standards and Best Practices into a Unified Framework."[29] It comes with 58 recommendations across 34 topic areas, distilled from 52 different sources. There's a lot of fantastic information in there. But please, make it stop.

What frameworks like the ones reviewed and offered in that report don't tell you is who should do what, when they should do it, and how they should do it. There's no guidance on how to implement all of the recommendations, let alone how to do so at scale in a timely fashion, nor how to update practices as the technology continues to evolve. Their recommendations require significant organizational change with no sense of how big the lift is, how to pull it off, or what the probability is of failure. Nor is there any kind of ranking on how to assess what to tackle first and/or how to prioritize everything else.

This is precisely where The Ethical Nightmare Challenge comes in. It's not only a framework. It's a *method* that is:

1. **Outcome oriented:** we need a clear sense of the desired outcome to define what success and failure looks like

2. **Readily deployable:** we can't wait months let alone years to implement nightmare avoidance strategies

3. **Dynamic and easy to update:** we can't adopt a rigid solution that can't adapt to technological, regulatory, and organizational changes

4. **Efficient:** we can't allow the solution to be delayed due to bottlenecks nor become the bottleneck itself

5. **Conducive to communication and collaboration across all levels of an organization:** we can't allow the solution to ignore the vast network of team interdependencies that characterizes agentic AI

At the core of The Ethical Nightmare Challenge as method is the seeding and spreading of loosely networked *ENC teams*. ENC teams are created on an as-needed basis throughout the organization. All teams use the same methods for nightmare avoidance.

To get a grip on what this looks like and why The Ethical Nightmare Challenge method satisfies all five of the above criteria, we'll look at ENC teams at three different levels of the organization: the project/AI solution level, the departmental level, and the C-suite/board level. We'll start in the middle and work our way out. I'll explain how these teams operate, what tools they need, and how this approach solves our problems.

Three Types of ENC Teams

The ENC Method has 7 steps. Here they are at a high level.

Step 1: Create an ENC team

Step 2: Ensure baseline knowledge of AI ethical risks and the ENC method

Step 3: Identify and score AI ethical nightmares

Step 4: Identify needed resources and training to avoid those nightmares

Step 5: Assign responsibilities for resource/training creation/delivery

Step 6: Assess progress

Step 7: Repeat as needed

The 7-Step ENC Method

Step #	Step Name	What You Do	Time
1.	Create the ENC team	Assemble 5–8 people (12 max) with cross-functional expertise, including at least one technologist. Leader sends invites.	1–2 weeks
2.	Ensure baseline knowledge of AI ethical risks and the ENC method	Team members complete ~1 hour of training on AI ethical risks and the ENC method. Can be done async or in-person.	~2 weeks
3.	Identify and score AI ethical ethical nightmares	Brainstorm AI ethical nightmares and their sources. Score each by probability and severity. High score = high priority.	30 min– few hours (across meetings)
4.	Identify needed resources and training to avoid those nightmares	Collaboratively identify what resources and training will contribute to nightmare avoidance.	30 min– few hours
5.	Assign responsibilities for resource/training creation/delivery	Assign a named person to own each resource or training initiative. Set target rollout and completion dates.	15–20 min
6.	Assess progress	Reconvene to check whether nightmare scores have sufficiently dropped. Refine resources/training if needed.	Brief meeting; time varies
7.	Repeat as needed	Revisit when AI evolves, new nightmares emerge, regulations change, or personnel turns over. Can disband if nothing new warrants action.	As needed

As we'll see, this method is used by every team, regardless of whether they operate at the enterprise-, department- or division-, or AI project level. That kind of methodological consistency in how AI nightmares are avoided translates to ease of communication and collaboration across the enterprise from top to bottom. Let's see how.

ENC Team #1: Department level

A VP of marketing for a Fortune 500 company is keen on scaling AI within her division. But she wants to ensure that things don't go sideways. Time for the ENC method.

Step 1: Create the ENC team

The marketing VP creates a team, including but not limited to members of her division. She will include those with traditional marketing experience as well as at least one technologist that is familiar with technical measures for AI risk mitigation and a technologist (it may be the same person) who is a project leader on AI marketing solutions. She may also include members from other departments, such as someone from product, someone from operations, perhaps a VP of marketing for a division other than her own. She is the ENC Team Leader.

How long does it take to create a team? We're talking about a week or two. Send some emails or Slack messages, get on the phone, hop on a video call. You're looking for 5–8 people, 12 max, since more than that is not only overkill, it slows down efficient meetings.

Step 2: Ensure baseline knowledge of AI ethical risks and the ENC method

The ENC Team Leader confirms the team is trained on:

- The basics of the ethical risks of AI (for example, the kind of information articulated in Chapters 1–3)

- The basics of the Ethical Nightmare Challenge method and associated tools (more on this, below)

In some cases, this kind of basic training will have been already provided. In others, an ENC Team Leader will have to ensure that team members get the requisite training. This training can be done in-person or asynchronously, or a combination of the two.

In my experience, if the training programs are ready—my firm offers asynchronous training for both the basics of the ethical risks of AI and the basics of ENC—giving people around 2 weeks to complete the training is enough. Give them much more time and procrastination gives way to forgetting about it altogether. Give them less and people can't find the time in their schedules. The key here is that baseline training is relatively brief—about an hour—so there's no large upfront commitment that stands as a blocker to participation.

Step 3: Identify and score AI ethical nightmares

The ENC team answers the first question of the Ethical Nightmare Challenge:

What are the marketing department's ethical nightmares pertaining to our current and near-future use of AI?

There are a variety of ways to answer this question. The team may do a whiteboarding/brainstorming session. They may—although I would rather burn in hell for eternity—write ideas on sticky notes they affix to a wall. They can contribute ideas in a shared doc asynchronously and then discuss live. They can even use an LLM as a sounding board and idea generator. But whatever they do, the team better not spend time creating an attractive PowerPoint presentation summarizing all of it. I'm begging you. In this context, functional and efficient beats beautiful every time.

It's important to note two related ideas here. First, remember that some potential nightmares are built into AI: the ones we discussed in Chapter 1 (such as bias, privacy violations, hallucinations, and automation bias) and Chapter 3 (such as snowball effects/cascading failures, emergent/system risks, and autonomy). ENC teams would do well to start there. Second, ENC teams need to not only think about what the nightmares are but also consider their sources. How might the department accidentally release marketing material with hallucinated content about a product? How might the department inadvertently release racist imagery while A/B testing with AI-generated content? And so on.

Listing potential nightmares and their sources is one thing. Prioritizing them is another. Thus, their next task is to give each nightmare a *nightmare score.*

There are a variety of ways to do this as well, the most basic being assigning a numerical score to the probability of the nightmare becoming a reality and the severity of the impact were that nightmare to become reality. High probability of hallucinating diagnoses in oncology ward = high nightmare score. Low probability of causing mental distress due to a plethora of options in e-commerce = low nightmare score.

I recommend to all clients that they first brainstorm potential ethical nightmares and subsequently assign nightmare scores. Otherwise, one person may raise a potential nightmare, another person says, "Yeah, but that's so unlikely" and then they're off on a different conversation. That conversation needs to be had, but not yet. First just get the nightmares on the table. Score afterward. Depending on the complexity of the AI under discussion, this can take anywhere from 30 minutes to a few hours, usually spread across a handful of meetings.

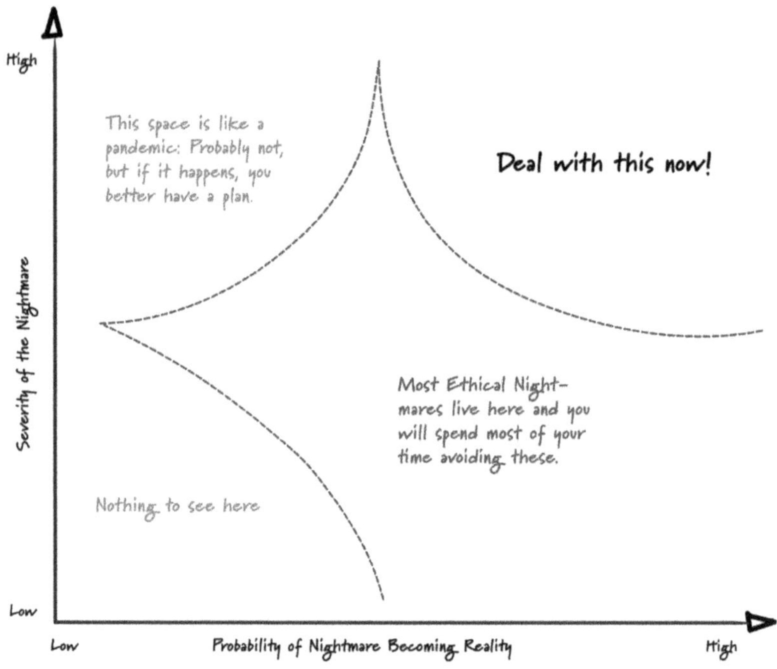

Step 4: Identify needed resources and training to avoid those nightmares

Now that the team has AI ethical nightmares and nightmare scores, it's time for the next two questions of the ENC:

What resources does the marketing department have to avoid those nightmares?

What kind of training do marketing personnel need so they can use those resources effectively?

This is a *collaborative problem-solving process*. The ENC team is thinking through how they currently handle issues; what tools they already have at their disposal; who they may reach out to within the organization that may have experience with this sort of thing; what governance structures and guidance already exist; where, when, and how they can best communicate information to various stakeholders, and so on. This isn't compliance, let alone compliance theater. To repeat the already italicized idea above, and I'll italicize it again for super emphasis, this is *collaborative, cross-functional problem-solving*.

I want to be clear about what problem the ENC team is solving. This is at the department level, so they are not themselves building AI solutions. The department is the organizing and governing structure under which AI project teams build AI solutions, where those solutions could lead to ethical nightmares for the department. In thinking about what's needed, they're asking: what resources and/or training can we provide our AI project teams with so that they'll avoid the identified ethical nightmares?

It may well be that certain *rules* or departmental policy will be of help. But a policy is only one tool among many for nightmare avoidance; there are loads of possibilities here. The ENC team may create weekly sessions in which project leaders exchange experiences and ideas about how they engage in ethical nightmare avoidance on their projects. Or maybe once a month a newsletter is sent out to all project leaders or everyone in the department to tell the story of one particularly clever and/or impactful nightmare avoidance strategy an AI project team successfully executed. Or maybe it explains how a nightmare avoidance strategy failed and reviews the lessons learned.

The ENC team is a problem-solver, not a god atop Mount Olympus hurling commandments to the mortals. Its workings *enable* AI project leaders and their teams to do *their* best in problem-solving for the AI solution they're working on (more about this soon). It's also worth highlighting that at least one member of this team is an AI project leader in the marketing department. That person should have enough on-the-ground experience to meaningfully contribute to conversations about what may plausibly (not) work for project leaders across the department. This is one reason why cross-functional membership of the ENC team is so important. We're not being "inclusive" for the sake of virtue signaling We're being inclusive because we need the insights of different people on the team if we're going to engage in efficient and effective problem-solving.

How long this step takes depends on the size of the department and the kind of AI it uses or will use soon. Once again, 30 minutes to a few hours is about right.

Step 5: Assign responsibilities for resource/training creation/delivery

The ENC team identifies who will own the various initiatives related to the resources and/or training that needs to be developed and delivered. Target dates for rollout and completion of those initiatives will also be set.

Suppose, for instance, the ENC team concludes in Step 3 that, among other things, a major source of its ethical nightmares is simply for marketing employees to be ignorant of the ways in which marketing content can become biased if left to an AI alone. After all, if employees don't know what AI disasters they must avoid and they regularly use AI, you've got dangerous employees on your hands. In Step 3 this is determined to be a high priority, and the ENC team's plan is to run an AI ethical nightmare-awareness campaign within the marketing department. They have also decided that they want 95% of marketing employees to be aware of the ethical nightmares of AI by the close of the next quarter; they think that's a sufficient threshold for blocking off this path to an ethical nightmare.

That campaign can take a variety of forms depending on how their department operates. It can be anywhere from formal training to a meeting that managers have with their direct reports to AI-generated videos that are sent around via email. Success can be measured in a variety of ways, ranging from the percentage of marketing employees who have received formal training to those that attended a meeting in which their team leader discussed ethical nightmares to the percentage of employees who viewed the entirety of the AI-generated videos to surveys distributed to targeted subsets of employees.

If it's not already obvious: there isn't one right way to do this.

Finally, in Step 5, the ENC team puts a particular person in charge of the ethical nightmare awareness campaign and identifies target rollout and completion dates.

How long does it take to assign these responsibilities? I don't know—15–20 minutes? It should be clear who does what given the resources that need to be created and the role and responsibilities of those on the ENC team. You're not going to tell someone in operations to add an adapter to a generative AI, after all.

Step 6: Assess progress

At the appropriate times, as determined in advance by the ENC leader with the advice of members, the ENC team meets to assess their progress. What you're looking for here is whether the resources and/or additional training sufficiently lowered the probability of the ethical nightmare occurring. After all, you can't change the severity of it, but you can reduce the likelihood, which in turn reduces the nightmare score.

If, for instance, you relied on people watching a 20-minute video and only 10% of people did, it may be that people weren't sufficiently aware of the video, or it was bad, or you failed to communicate how important it was that people watch it. As such, the likelihood of the ethical nightmare hasn't been sufficiently reduced. Should you abandon the video or double down? That's a team decision. Step 6 is complete once it's been decided whether the nightmare scores are low enough to proceed or if resources and/or training need to be refined and/or added. In some cases, if the nightmare score is too high and the resources aren't available to reduce them, putting the project on pause is the not-reckless move.

Assessing progress shouldn't take very long since it's primarily a matter of revising the earlier likelihood score. And if you've done a good job defining what a successful resource looks like during Step 4, it's all the easier. The time-consuming part isn't the team meetings, it's creating the resources and/or training needed to avoid ethical nightmares. That's as it should be; less time talking, more time doing.

Step 7: Repeat as needed

At appropriate times, the marketing ENC team leader determines whether repeating the earlier steps is warranted.

What are appropriate times? This can be defined formally or informally. Formal would entail that it occurs on a regularly scheduled basis, such as biannually, annually, etc. In those cases, the ENC team would reconvene and assess the state of the division in relation to its present and near-future use of AI as well as the state of AI progress more generally. If nothing has happened—there are no new kinds of AI, there are no new ethical nightmares, there are no new ways of realizing familiar nightmares, there are no relevant personnel changes, etc.—that can be determined in short order. The team may decide that there's no need to reperform The Ethical Nightmare Challenge and they disband until the next scheduled time. If something has happened—a new bias or hallucination mitigation tool has been invented that would help all project teams, a new powerful AI marketing tool has been released—then checking to see whether current resources/training are still adequate or whether updates are needed is warranted.

The informal way of doing this entails no scheduled/predetermined times when the ENC team reconvenes. Instead, members of the team, including but not limited to the leader, may realize change is afoot and/or see things on the ground that indicate taking The Ethical Nightmare Challenge again is called for, or should at least be considered. For instance, the AI project leader on the team may have seen firsthand that certain resources or knowledge is consistently absent in the projects he leads. He also knows he's not the only one; colleagues who are also project leaders are noticing the same thing. At that point he may talk to/email/text/slack/whatever the ENC team leader to tell her it's time to get the gang back together. His on-the-ground experience helps the leader understand the needs of the division.

The formal and informal approaches are compatible. An organization can allow for both: scheduled meetings plus ad-hoc meetings when the ENC team leader thinks it's warranted based on talking to other members of the team. I'm not interested in getting too prescriptive here.

Throughout these steps you may have noticed the process is:

- Oriented around avoiding defined (ethically, reputationally, legally) bad outcomes

- Readily actionable; it does not depend upon a drawn-out design phase. The ENC team is getting to work as fast as reasonably possible. The biggest obstacle is relatively small: basic training on AI nightmares and the ENC process.

- Adaptable to advances in AI and changes in regulatory context; whatever comes down the line, the operating model remains constant.

- Not dependent on clearing a bottleneck nor does the process become a bottleneck itself. The marketing department doesn't need to wait for enterprise-wide policy or guidance (remember what I was screaming in the Introduction?). There is also nothing that would require them to become a bottleneck, which will become even clearer as we consider the next ENC team.

- Conducive to communication and collaboration across the organization. It includes a VP of marketing, who reports to perhaps the enterprise-wide CMO or the COO, direct reports of the VP, a VP of marketing from another division, a project leader, a data scientist or two, and so on. We're at the starting point of creating a web.

When you add up all the time it takes to engage in the process, not counting the time it takes to develop the right resources and/or training, we're talking about something that takes weeks or a few months to implement, not years. Yes, building things takes time and there's nothing one can do about that. But going from zero to having effectively implemented AI ethical nightmare avoidance in a few months is a game changer compared to the C-suite-bottlenecked, years-long standard approach.

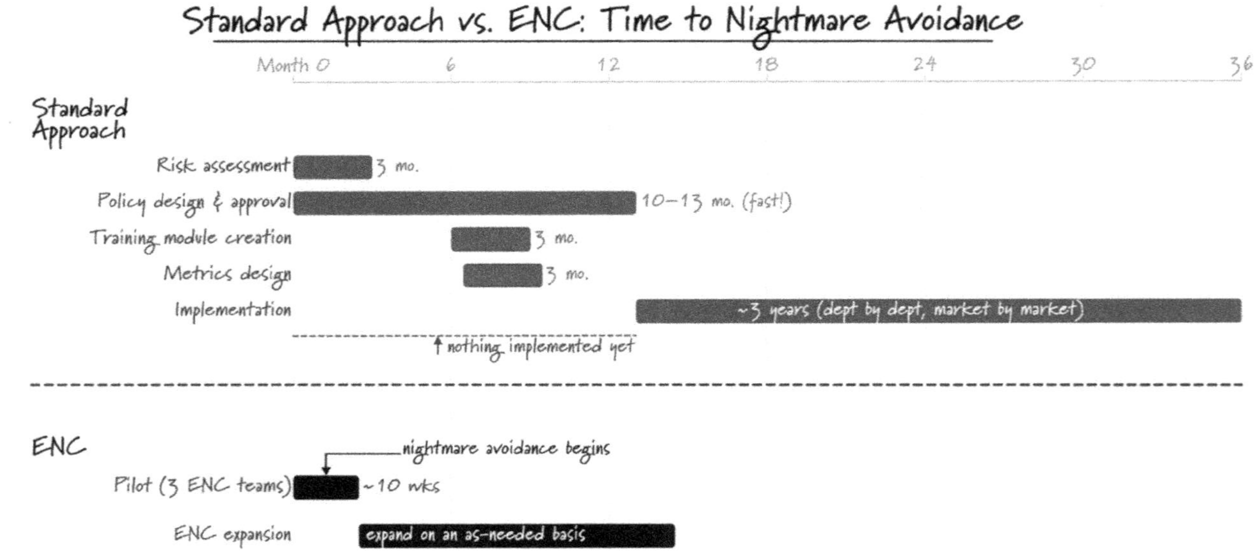
Standard Approach vs. ENC: Time to Nightmare Avoidance
Month 0   6   12   18   24   30   36
Standard Approach
Risk assessment   3 mo.
Policy design & approval   10—13 mo. (fast!)
Training module creation   3 mo.
Metrics design   3 mo.
Implementation   ~3 years (dept by dept, market by market)
↑ nothing implemented yet
ENC
nightmare avoidance begins
Pilot (3 ENC teams)   ~10 wks
ENC expansion   expand on an as-needed basis

This ENC team exists somewhere in the middle of the organization. It's within marketing only, so it's more vertical than horizontal. In fact, if it's one division among, say, four marketing divisions, it's a narrow vertical band. But if that division covers the most important suite of products within the company, this ENC team packs a powerful punch.

From here let's go deeper into the division, to the project level, after which we'll head back upstairs to the C-suite and board.

ENC Team #2: AI project level

Imagine a project leader for an agentic AI. And let's say he's in the marketing department as well. He knows enough about AI's risks to realize that he needs to take The Ethical Nightmare Challenge. However! The marketing department ENC team we just discussed either doesn't exist yet or they're in the middle of their own work. They won't be of great help. What does he do?

He follows *exactly the same process as ENC Team #1*. It's worth repeating it here:

Step 1: Create the AI project-level ENC team

Step 2: Ensure baseline knowledge of AI ethical risks and the ENC method

Step 3: Identify and score project-specific AI ethical nightmares

Step 4: Identify needed resources and training to avoid those nightmares

Step 5: Assign responsibilities for resource/training creation/delivery

Step 6: Assess progress

Step 7: Repeat as needed

Because at this level we're more focused on developers and end users, it's critical to highlight the importance of the cross-functionality of the ENC team. It's also worth noting that the resources/training we're identifying at this level may be for the project team *and/or* end users of the solution. The data scientists will see technical sources of nightmares and technical resources needed to mitigate those risks. The marketer will have insight into sources of nightmares related to how consumers behave to which engineers may be blind. In some cases, the technical source of the risk may need a non-technical solution. For instance, given that hallucinations are inevitable and there's only so much data scientists can do to decrease them, the nightmares that may result must be mitigated in a non-technical way. Non-technical mitigation examples might include training end users to be sensitive to hallucinations and understanding when fact-checking is crucial and who should conduct it. In other cases, nightmares may manifest via consumer behavior and preferences. A generative AI that creates racially offensive images is a marketer's nightmare for which, at least in some cases, there will be technical fixes. And in still other cases there will be a mix of technical and non-technical ways to avoid the nightmares.

What enables this motley crew to work together? They're speaking the same language, the language of nightmares. And each member understands that different members of the team have different superpowers that enable them to see nightmares they may not have seen themselves and to deploy resources that they may not have known about or had authority to use. We are creating a web of technologists and non-technologists who collaboratively identify and avoid AI ethical nightmares at the project level. People who serve on these ENC teams will, of course, also be great members of department- and even enterprise-wide ENC teams.

Throughout these steps you may have noticed all the things we noticed about ENC team #1. It is outcome oriented, readily actionable, adaptable to AI advances and regulatory contexts, and isn't dependent on, or a source of, bottlenecks. It's true that this ENC team would *benefit* from existing inside a division that has taken The Ethical Nightmare Challenge, but they don't *need* it to get to work. In fact, perhaps this is the department's first significant use of AI outside of CoPilot. Perhaps this team exists inside a startup that lacks robust departments (or the marketing department is literally one person). The ENC team approach works all the same at the project level.

Let me repeat the benefit of having a department or division (not just project teams) engage in the ENC and what this says about the essential *function* of departments in this context. The department-level ENC is there to *create the resources and the environment of trained personnel so that project leaders engaged in ENC efforts can be more successful.* Department ENC teams are engaged in capacity building. They are not, or at least not primarily, creating rigid rules or commandments. They are not providing SOPs with which they expect compliance. They are giving their teams the resources they need to responsibly develop and use AI at scale.

Ok, back in the elevator, heading up.

ENC Team #3: The board and C-suite

I think you already know what's coming: this is the same 7-step process the department engaged in. This is, after all, one reason the ENC is so effective: its portability. And just as the department has the function of enabling project leaders and employees rise to The Ethical Nightmare Challenge, the C-suite and board has the function of helping departments rise to The Ethical Nightmare Challenge. Again, this is not, or not primarily, issuing edicts from atop Mount Olympus. This is enabling departments/divisions to avoid their respective nightmares, which in turn enables their project leaders to avoid their nightmares.

There is, however, one place they need to focus that departments do not: the ethical nightmares that arise due to interdependencies and breaks in the system. It's one thing for marketing or HR or finance to work within their departments and avoid ethical nightmares. It's another when AI travels across departmental boundaries, leading to sources of risk that result from breakdowns in communication and/or collaboration. Some of the key questions the enterprise-wide ENC team needs to answer include:

- What ethical nightmares could result from breakdowns within and across divisions of the enterprise?

- What resources do they need to increase cross-department/division communication and collaboration?

- What sort of training do they need to use those resources effectively?

The need to answer these questions echoes something we saw in the department ENC team: the board/C-suite level team needs to include people who can help them solve their problems, including division heads (ideally those who have participated in and/or lead ENC teams themselves), as well as AI project leaders who can help senior executives see what's happening on the ground and what plausible solutions look like.

As for when and how often this senior executive team should take The Ethical Nightmare Challenge, we have the same formal and informal approaches we saw with department ENC teams.

ENC Teams as Emergency Response

ENC teams are focused on nightmare avoidance. But one of the lessons we learned in our travels from narrow, through generative, and to agentic/clusterfuck AI is that there is SO MUCH UNPREDICTABILITY. Nor can we wrap our heads around all the various interdependencies of the complex software ecosystems that constitute agentic AI. This leads us to the unsettling conclusion that *bad things will happen.*

We saw a glimpse of this in Chapter 4 where I quoted General McChrystal's *Team of Teams*. Airplanes have become so complex with so many interdependent parts that it's impossible to predict all the things that could go wrong let alone devise procedures for dealing with each one of those problems. Or to take another example from his book:

> A checklist is inadequate for surgery because of the quintillions of possibilities that interdependence generates. We would never call the rigors of medical school "easy," but it is more feasible to spend seven years learning about the complex cause and effect relationships in the human body than to attempt to record and memorize every possible event that can befall bodies.[30]

This shouldn't lead us to despair. It just means we need to place a great deal of weight on incident *detection*. Monitoring the AI and responding appropriately in a timely fashion is crucial. This means there are two additional tasks a project-level ENC team should engage in.

First, as part of the resources they create to avoid potential nightmares, they should create and/or identify what resources will be used to detect ethical nightmares beginning to unfold. "For this solution," they should ask themselves, "what are the red lights we have to install for when things start breaking, preferably before a crash?"

Second, they should at least be a part of, if not lead, incident response measures if the detection comes too late and/or it wasn't spotted at all. They are, after all, project-specific subject matter experts on what ethical nightmares had previously been identified and what resources have already been deployed to avoid them. They are in the best position of anyone to identify appropriate solutions to an (emerging) ethical AI nightmare.

Tools for Teams

I've articulated seven steps ENC teams take to carry out their respective missions. But we need to add more to this structure. While it is true that everyone engaging in those steps does a tremendous amount to fuel communication and collaboration, we need more. More specifically, we need them using similar tools to create greater consistency in how ethical AI nightmares are identified, scored, and prioritized.

There are three such tools worth emphasizing.

The first tool is simply a brief questionnaire, primarily completed by the potential ENC team leader, as to whether an ENC team should be created in the first place. This will depend on several factors, including a general sense of what's at stake if things go wrong. These questions can be customized in various ways, but here are five good candidates to start with:

- Does this AI make decisions that could significantly affect the well-being of our customers/clients and/or employees and/or investors? Could it potentially violate their rights?

- Could failure create significant reputational, legal, or financial consequences? (Or more specifically, could failure lead to a loss of $X or more?)

- Does this AI cross departmental boundaries or touch sensitive data?

- Is this a new type of AI for our organization?

- How bad would it be if this AI manifested the familiar AI ethical risks, such as those related to bias, privacy violations, and hallucinations?

Once again, organizations can be formal or informal about this. A formal approach would be something like, "If two or more questions receive a 'yes', an ENC team should be formed." The informal approach would be closer to, "Leaders are expected to answer these questions as best they can and make their best professional judgment as to why those answers indicate the need (or not) for an ENC team." Formal or informal, the results of the questionnaire should be documented.

The second tool helps the ENC leader think about who should be on the team. Strict criteria are not necessary. Instead, the goal is to use questions that enable the ENC leader to exercise their professional judgment in an informed way. It's worth highlighting here that ENC leaders do not and, in some cases, should not, restrict membership to employees. Having a member from the company from whom they are licensing an AI—say, a data scientist from OpenAI or Google or Microsoft or Anthropic, etc.—can be an extremely useful addition. Similarly, if, say, a project-level ENC team is building an AI solution for a client, having people from the client side serve on the ENC team is, all else equal, a great idea.

The third and perhaps most important tool helps the ENC team at each part of the 7-step method. In my practice, we provide clients with enterprise, department, and project ENC team worksheets that guide and document the 7 steps they take. Because each worksheet is nearly identical in structure, anyone who has seen one ENC worksheet can pick up a second one from another team, regardless of where that team sits in the organizational hierarchy, and immediately understand what they're looking at. A C-suite executive or board director, for instance, if they've served on an ENC team, can pick up the ENC worksheet of a particular AI project and readily interpret what ethical nightmares were identified, how they were scored, what resources were developed, etc.

Crucially, when the same methods and tools are used across enterprise, department, and project teams, a great deal is done to facilitate communication. What's more, consistency in method, tools, and documentation make for straightforward ways to conduct assessments of how well your ENC teams are doing the jobs they are intended to do.

ENC Teams in Bloom

Each ENC team has marching orders by which they carry out their respective missions, no matter what level of the organization they operate at. The teams themselves foster communication and collaboration across the organization by virtue of the membership being composed of diverse members of the organization. What's more, as ENC teams form and disband and form again as needed, and as different ENC teams have different members, each ENC team is a locus of cross-functional and cross-departmental communication and collaboration. Each ENC team is itself a web of interconnectivity, and as the ENC teams increase in number over months and years, the interconnectivity of all those people across all those teams increase as well. We're not just building nightmare avoidance solutions. We're building an organizational *capacity* and a *culture* of nightmare avoidance.

But it doesn't stop there. The interconnectivity doesn't only exist within teams but across the teams themselves.

Suppose, for instance, the C-suite ENC team understands it needs to create the means by which departments collaborate so that nothing falls between the cracks. They may be concerned that AI agents in different departments may act in an uncoordinated way, leading to snowball effects/cascading failures and systemic/emergent risks. They want to coordinate interdepartmental means of communication and collaboration about AI ethical nightmares so that interdepartmental AI agents can communicate and collaborate without ethical nightmares rearing their heads. Maybe they create opportunities—for example, a workshop or a discussion forum—for ENC leaders of different departments and/or divisions to share what they've learned, where they succeeded, where they failed, and so forth. "Here's how we avoided this nightmare. We're not sure how to avoid this other one, though; any ideas or experience with this?" Or perhaps the C-suite creates an interdepartmental ENC SWAT team that starts by asking: "What are the ethical nightmares that could emerge from these different agents interacting across all these departments? What cross-departmental resources can we use to avoid those ethical nightmares? What training will people need to use those resources effectively?" That ENC SWAT team would surely have ENC project leaders of those agents included in the team.

The C-suite may provide other common resources that all ENC teams can pull from, like an organization-specific ethical

AI nightmare inventory or nightmare-avoidance strategies that teams have found particularly useful and applicable in multiple scenarios. Similarly, a department level ENC team may provide a resource by which project-level ENC teams can learn about the latest in nightmare identification and avoidance given changing technology and advances in research.

At the core of the standard approach is compliance with stale policies. At the core of the ENC teams approach is a culture and practice of dynamic, collaborative problem-solving.

There's no real choice here. Start forming your ENC teams.

7

ENC: An Approach So Flexible It Makes Simone Biles Look Like C-3PO

One lesson we've learned is that AI, especially agentic AI, is built and modified by dozens and maybe even hundreds of teams across multiple organizations. If we're to avoid AI's ethical nightmares, we need to do our best to make communication and collaboration across these teams as easy as possible. What's more, since there are so many teams using so many different AIs throughout a single company, getting everyone to think about, talk about, and address ethical nightmares in the same way is crucial. As General McChrystal put it in *Team of Teams*, we want all these different people to manifest a "shared consciousness." Consistent, simple messaging and consistent practices are thus keystones in the overall nightmare avoidance endeavor. Get it wrong—have people speaking different languages and engaging in fundamentally different practices—and you'll have chaos.

Given this, and despite my being generally allergic to rules and discipline (I was once fired for insubordination as a lifeguard), I must insist on some requirements for how an organization rises to the Ethical Nightmare Challenge. At the same time, I'm not interested in being a dictator. Some aspects of how to create and implement ENC teams are your call. You know your organization, you know your company, you know better than I do what will work there.

In this chapter, I'll lay out what's negotiable and what's non-negotiable when adopting the Ethical Nightmare Challenge. And for all you top-down governance people wondering how all this relates to you and your work and *am I seriously and recklessly suggesting we don't need robust corporate governance because I'm a know-nothing and how dare I undermine your important work and...* don't worry. I have something for you, too.

Hands Off!

Here are the things every organization should adhere to with draconian rigor when taking on the Ethical Nightmare Challenge.

The Three Questions

Everyone—board/C-suite, departments, project leaders—should all lead with the three questions:

1. What are our AI ethical nightmares?

2. What resources do we need to avoid them?

3. How do we train our people to use those resources effectively?

(There's a good reason you're seeing this repeatedly. Repetition creates habits, habits create culture. The repetition also speaks to how important it is to keep to this simple, universal approach to avoiding breakdowns in communication and thus collaboration). If you're in the C-suite and these questions are drilled into your head, and you know they're in your department and project leaders' heads, you know how to have the risk conversation. You ask them the three questions. They should have answers ready for you. In fact, they should be ready to share an ENC worksheet with you. If they don't have answers for how to avoid nightmares, you shouldn't sleep well.

Suppose you're a project leader and you hear from your boss or read in an email or are told in the cafeteria line that executives are worried about some specific ethical nightmare and so they've provided you with resources A and B and training modules X and Y to help you avoid those nightmares. You already have a mental model of how to take on this information. It's just of a piece with what you do with your team on a regular basis.

You need to talk to a third-party vendor because you're in procurement? Ask them. "We need you to answer these three questions. Please provide documentation for verification. That's how we do things here."

You're a leader in HR and you've brought in a new AI tool for HR personnel to use? You tell them how the builders of that tool—whether it was built in-house or procured from a third-party—answered the three questions. Those people immediately understand what nightmares were identified, what resources are available for avoiding them, and whether they need any kind of training to use the tool/resources effectively.

When the three questions are echoed here and there and everywhere by everyone, this does a tremendous amount to build consistency, mutual understanding, and thereby collaboration. You're not just giving instructions with which people must comply. You're giving everyone the simple and common framework they need to understand what's going on. You're building both an organizational capacity distributed across all employees and a culture that takes ethical nightmare avoidance seriously.

The 7-Step Method

The three questions establish what questions need to be answered and the 7-step method establishes *how* to answer those questions. Recall the 7 steps (repetition creates habit...):

1. Create an ENC team

2. Ensure baseline knowledge of AI ethical risks and the ENC method

3. Identify and score AI ethical nightmares

4. Identify needed resources and training to avoid those nightmares

5. Assign responsibilities for resource/training creation/delivery

6. Assess progress

7. Repeat as needed

I don't care if you're on the board or the Chief Information Officer or the VP of marketing or the project lead for an agentic AI solution—*if you don't follow these steps, I will strike down upon you with great vengeance and fury.*

Again, this consistency across teams makes communication and collaboration possible. If you've served on one ENC team then you know how the second team will operate, and the third one, and so on. That holds if all three ENC teams you serve on are at the same level or if they're at different levels of the organization.

Suppose you're at the department level and you learn that an enterprise ENC team has made decisions that impact your department. You know, at the procedural level, how they came to those conclusions. You also know what success looks like, since nightmare scores have been identified and shared with you, and you know who owns the creation of the resource/delivery of the requisite training. Similarly, if you've just caught wind that there's an enterprise ENC team doing its work, you understand what they're doing and how they're doing it. This level of transparency and consistency plays a huge role in creating reliable and predictable ways of operating in a complex and turbulent environment.

Cross-Functional/Departmental Membership

Ok, look. I'll be honest. Slogans like, "Our diversity is our strength!" make me a bit nauseous. But don't get me wrong: ethically speaking it sounds mostly right, although I prefer the less pithy but more accurate "Our diversity is one of our strengths alongside others." In the case of ENC teams, this is certainly true.

There are, of course, different kinds of diversity. *At a minimum* we need a diversity of expertise/business experience. ENC teams can't just be composed of engineers and data scientists. Nor can they only be composed of people within one business function like HR or marketing. As explained in the previous chapter, different roles can see different nightmares and different ways of avoiding those nightmares. In most cases, nightmare avoidance will require a suite of technical and human-related tools (for example, a human/team in the loop). The product member of the ENC team may have product design modifications that will encourage certain user behaviors, the developer may have a way of tweaking the AI (such as adding an adapter), the marketing member may explain how this impacts how the product is advertised, and so on.

Other kinds of diversity are helpful, if not extremely helpful. Many people will reasonably bristle at ENC teams that are demographically homogenous. An ENC team of all middle-aged white men introduces the possibility if not probability of blind spots. That said, a team solely comprised of young Asian women will also introduce the possibility if not probability of a different set of blind spots. This constitutes strong reason to take great care in creating ENC teams, which brings us to the next nonnegotiable.

Use of Nearly-Identical Tools and Templates

There are the three questions that specify what needs to be answered. Then there's the 7-step method that explains how to answer those questions. We also discussed who needs to engage in those 7 steps. But more must be standardized.

Tools and templates are needed throughout the 7-step process: how to create teams, what baseline education about AI risks is delivered, how nightmare scores are determined and recorded, and so on. If you've seen one set of ENC-generated documents, you've seen them all, at least in terms of the structure of those documents. The content will vary, of course.

This means that when an executive who serves on an enterprise ENC team looks at the materials generated by a project level ENC team, she knows exactly what she's looking at. She sees how the team was formed, she sees how baseline knowledge was established, she sees the nightmare scores of various ethical nightmares that pertain to the project, and so on. She is accustomed to seeing nightmares of the enterprise as opposed to those of a particular project, but since she understands the structure, the content of the project-level ENC assessments is readily accessible.

On the other hand, if different teams have different methods of nightmare avoidance and different methods for recording their efforts, a breakdown in communication and (thus) chaos will ensue.

You Do You

But again, I'm no king! There are all sorts of ways ENC teams can and *should* be bent without breaking. The ways they can bend constitute a strength; the adaptability of ENC teams is one of their greatest virtues in the relentless morphing of the technological and regulatory landscape. Of the ceaseless, tireless transmogrification of the AI industrial comp… ok I'm getting carried away.

Scope of Risks

Throughout this book I've focused on ethical risks, although I've also mentioned reputational and legal risks. There is, of course, a Venn diagram that one could draw here, but must I?

There are other risks one could incorporate into the responsibility of an ENC team. They could also consider cybersecurity or operational risks, for instance. After all, most Responsible AI programs include commitments to "security" and "privacy." For some organizations, including cyber risks within the scope of an ENC team makes a lot of sense. For others, not so much.

One thing I've learned in my work with clients is that every company has its own quirks and features and particular weirdness. In some cases, my team and I were brought in by the Chief Information Officer (CIO) or the CISO. In others, it was the Chief Compliance Officer or Director of Compliance for a division, and they and the cyber teams are siloed. They do their work, the cyber team does theirs, but there isn't much interaction between the two. In still other cases we were brought in by people with titles like "Global

Head of Responsible AI" and their teams were not integrated closely with cybersecurity *or* compliance.

Now I could tell you what the *ideal* is: everyone should work together and be integrated and there should be no silos. But we shouldn't let perfect be the enemy of the good. If you're looking to create ENC teams and you're the head of marketing and you have very little interaction with the cyber folks, I wouldn't make it a requirement that the ENC team scope includes cyber risks. *Start with the lightest political lift to get things started.* As your AI risk practice matures, you can integrate cyber risks into your ENC team. On the other hand, if cyber teams are already well integrated with the work, then it makes sense to include them in the scope of ENC teams now.

Content of Regulatory and/or Cultural Standards

I've pointed out that nightmares vary across departments and roles. The ethical nightmares of the C-suite and board are different from those of HR, even if there's overlap. But of course there are different ethical nightmares depending upon *where* the AI is deployed. Different markets have different regulatory standards. Different countries have different cultural standards.

In identifying ethical nightmares, ENC teams can tailor those nightmares to where they operate. There might be some ethical nightmares that pertain to operating in France (they're a sensitive bunch, non?) that don't apply to the U.S. There are regulations that apply in nanny-state California that don't apply in kill-or-be-killed Texas. ENC teams are not tied to specific procedures that relate to specific regulations. That's crucial, since the regulatory landscape is constantly shifting (an executive order on AI can be here one day and gone the next!). In fact, that means ENC teams *absolutely should not* be tied to a certain regulatory standard. They need to be adaptable to the changing environment, capable of recognizing that new regulations have come along to which they must adhere. They need to be *quickly reactive* to new requirements, not welded to existing rails.

Kinds of Technology

There's a giant "AI" on the cover of this book. I've prattled on endlessly about this AI and that AI. So yes, let's focus on AI ethical nightmares. But there's nothing built into the ENC method that says those teams are only allowed to focus on AI.

As new technologies become relevant to an organization—it could be augmented and/or virtual reality, blockchain, quantum computers, and whatever they think of next—ENC teams are perfectly positioned to handle them. We don't have to go running back to the top-down, value-first standard approach that ends in a dead policy. Those technologies can be onboarded as quickly as it takes ENC teams to ensure baseline knowledge of those technologies and their attendant risks as part of step 2 of the ENC method.

Marrying ENC to Existing Practices

Every organization has a way of operating. A company has existing governance structures, policies, procedures, teams, and technologies. I've been referring to these things as "resources" of the organization. Implementing ENC teams thus requires a vision of how those teams integrate with those existing resources.

There are two ways of understanding what this integration looks like. One is to understand how existing resources fold into the ENC approach. The other is to understand how the ENC approach folds into existing resources. Let's start with the first one.

Folding Existing Resources into ENC Teams

Three existing resources can be helpful in integrating as part of your ENC process: existing Responsible AI (RAI) or AI Ethical Risk policies, existing RAI risk boards, and existing RAI frameworks. And a bonus: existing RAI software! We'll look at each in turn.

Existing RAI Policy

I explained in Chapter 4 why a Responsible AI/AI ethics policy can't be the foundation of an efficient and effective approach to ethical nightmare avoidance. Am I against them as such? In principle, I am not. If the C-suite/board level ENC team comes together, identifies nightmares, and decides that a crucial resource at their disposal is an enterprise-wide policy, well, fine. I'm skeptical about what it can accomplish unless, of course, the policy is to form ENC teams as needed. But whether to have a policy and what it should contain, once you've adopted the ENC approach, is a skirmish I would rather opt out of. For some organizations, it probably makes sense in some form or other, particularly for those that need to ban certain kinds of AI use. In other organizations, especially smaller ones like startups, it probably doesn't.

The main point, though, is that we should see policies, whether they are AI-specific or not, as one tool among many that organizations have at their disposal. And just like any tool, it may or may not make sense to use it. This means, among other things, that organizations with existing RAI policies do not need to start over or throw out their policy. It may well do a lot of good, important work. In that case, if there is an enterprise-wide policy, the ways that policy may be breached can simply be included among the identified nightmares in Step 3 of the ENC method; integration is straightforward.

Existing RAI Risk Boards

In *Ethical Machines* I wrote about the importance of an AI ethics committee. And every organization I've worked with, and those I haven't, have some form of risk board to which teams escalate what they deem as "high risk" AI. When it comes to narrow AI—which is the context in which I wrote that book—ethics committees made a lot of sense. They still make a lot of sense. But we need to rethink their place in the organization. They should be a backup when needed, not the default plan to address high risk AI.

The reason is simple: it's not scalable. As the quantity of AI use cases expands, the ethics committee cannot handle all of them. I have only ever seen ethics committees comprised primarily of senior-level personnel. They have their day jobs. Their committee work is a small fraction of what they do, and it cannot become their full-time jobs. And they need to be senior-level because they need the power and authority to veto projects or require effective risk mitigations to be introduced before the AI team is permitted to proceed to next stages. Further, in some cases, this committee must deal with AI that is procured from third parties. What's more, given the time it takes a committee of senior executives to become sufficiently knowledgeable about an AI use case, the ethics committee becomes a major bottleneck to innovation as various projects wait to be evaluated.

On the other hand, project-level ENC teams handle a vast majority of nightmare identification, avoidance, detection, and emergency response, even for high-risk AI. If they cannot figure out how to sufficiently mitigate the risks, then it probably makes sense to cancel the project. If for some reason canceling the project is disastrous, then it probably makes sense to escalate to a group of senior executives that constitute an enterprise AI risk committee. But this is the exception to the rule that ENC teams are best positioned to evaluate AI use cases for potential nightmares and to devise appropriate strategies for nightmare avoidance and response. So don't disband your existing AI risk board. See them as one resource among many that has a place while also being easily overburdened and a bottleneck. Use it wisely.

Existing RAI Frameworks

Some organizations have developed frameworks or guidelines that they find useful for assessing AI risks. For instance, one client of mine likes to create frameworks that he then names with an acronym that spells out a kind of animal: the WOLF framework for AI agents, for example. Other organizations have less fanciful frameworks that deal with issues pertaining to fairness or explainability or privacy.

How do such frameworks fit within The Ethical Nightmare Challenge? There are two ways to proceed here. The first is to simply take those guides/decision trees as among the *resources* your organization uses to avoid ethical nightmares; they are some of the answers to the second question of The Ethical Nightmare Challenge.

The second way is to simply let them go. For instance, instead of having a special framework or deliberative guide for thinking about the risks that pertain to agentic AI by virtue of their autonomy, you can just:

1. Identify what kinds of ethical nightmares are relevant to different levels of autonomy (for example, the extent to which the AI agent "checks in" with a person before it takes additional steps) and what the probability of those nightmares occurring is.

2. Identify and/or build the resources needed for avoiding and detecting those ethical nightmares related to each level of autonomy. (One useful thing to do here is to determine milestones the AI may reach such that you feel comfortable enhancing its autonomy.)

3. Train the people who will oversee the (low/medium/ high) autonomous agents.

Unsurprisingly, this second approach is my preferred way of going about things. We don't need special frameworks and deliberative guides for autonomy and privacy and hallucinations and… We just need to see that autonomy can be a source of ethical nightmares (along with cascading failures, systemic risks, etc.) and so it's something we need to pay attention to when we're identifying and scoring ethical nightmares in part 3 of the 7-step ENC method.

Existing RAI Software

One more note on resources I haven't discussed yet: AI governance/Responsible AI software. Some of that software is for data scientists to use at the model/solution level. For instance, there is software that assesses for bias or the rate of hallucination of an AI. Some software scans for sensitive data a user may input into the system via a prompt while other software may scan for sensitive data among the AI outputs. There is also risk and compliance software that may help companies track their inventory of AI throughout their enterprise as well as the extent to which those models comply with regulations and/or internal policy. In some cases, this kind of software comes from third-party vendors that specialize in Responsible AI. In other cases—in fact, in most cases with my clients—existing governance, risk, and compliance software is used and modified to include Responsible AI requirements.

There are two things to note here. First, software solutions are important resources. They are the kinds of resources that should be identified by an enterprise and/or department ENC team, keeping in mind that project level leaders should serve on those teams so they can provide their on-the-ground insights into what is needed and what will work.

Second, these solutions are never the entirety of the solution. As I hope to have demonstrated by now, nightmare avoidance is an exceedingly complex affair and no software, no matter how impressive it is, can handle all nightmare avoidance. Anyone who tells you otherwise is trying to sell you something (probably AI governance software).

Third, that software is a tool, a means to an end. It cannot tell you what the end is. On the other hand, the ENC approach starts with the end. It is an outcome oriented approach, as we've now discussed ad nauseum. The ENC approach thus gives you a basis on which to assess the utility of various software options: would use of X software bring nightmare scores down in a meaningful way? If yes, sounds like, all else equal (such as cost), you've got a good solution on your hands. If not, don't waste your money.

Folding ENC Teams into Existing Resources

The ENC approach is laser focused on building the organizational capacity to avoid nightmares at scale. In my estimation, it is the only viable method for this task. All existing alternatives, including the ones my team and I have built, pale in comparison in every respect.

ENC teams do not, however, do everything that needs to be done from an AI governance perspective. After all, at least in larger organizations, there are existing risk functions that can and should play a role. I'm thinking here of things like internal audit teams, legal and compliance teams, and executives who are responsible for giving the final green light. ENC teams do not replace their important work.

Internal compliance and audit teams, at a minimum, verify that the 7-step ENC method was carried out and documented. Above that, they can answer qualitative questions: did they identify the relevant nightmare scenarios or skip uncomfortable questions? Did they implement the resources they documented? Are their metrics meaningful or cosmetic?

Legal and compliance teams assess whether the nightmare-avoiding resources that were deployed are sufficient for regulatory compliance and commensurate with the organization's legal risk appetite. This is made easier if someone from legal/risk/compliance served on the project level ENC team.

Senior executives provide the green light after reviewing ENC team efforts and the approvals of audit, legal, and compliance.

ENC teams don't only integrate with these functions, though. They make those jobs easier in two respects: first, by doing the heavy lifting of nightmare identification and avoidance themselves, and second, by doing it in a way that consistently creates the sort of documentation those functions review.

Consider what typically happens today when legal or compliance gets involved with AI. They're brought in late—often when a project is nearly ready to deploy—and asked, "Hey, is this compliant?" (Same goes for cybersecurity teams; "We're shipping this next week—can you make sure it's secure?") They're forced to make quick judgments about technologies they may not fully understand, in contexts where the full scope of risks may not have been systematically identified. They become bottlenecks not because they're slow or bureaucratic—okay, fine, not *only* because they're slow or bureaucratic—but because they're being asked to assess risks that should have been identified and mitigated much earlier in the development process.

ENC teams flip this dynamic. Because project-level ENC teams are identifying nightmares from the beginning of development, and because these teams often *include* members from legal, compliance, and privacy, risk identification happens early and systematically. By the time a project reaches the point where it needs formal compliance review, ethical nightmare scenarios have already been scored, mitigated, and re-scored. Audit, compliance, etc. teams aren't scrambling to understand what could go wrong—they're validating that the preventive measures are adequate. (Note, though, that members of risk functions who serve on a project level ENC team cannot also be part of the risk team that validates their work; otherwise you have the fox guarding the henhouse.)

Finally, while project-level ENC teams are overseen by existing risk functions, as ENC maturity grows and ENC teams consistently prove themselves capable, increased responsibilities and authority can be granted to them. Perhaps in early days all ENC-generated materials are reviewed. Perhaps in middle days, those materials are randomly audited. Perhaps in much later days they can greenlight AI use cases/deployments themselves. In other words, the degree of autonomy and authority granted to ENC teams can evolve as ENC maturity increases.

Come to think of it, I suggest a nested modification of the ENC framework for ENC maturity:

1. Identify what kinds of ethical nightmares are relevant to each level of autonomy (for example, the extent to which the ENC team must check in with managers/executives before taking additional steps) and what the probability of those nightmares occurring is.

2. Identify what resources you have or will build for avoiding and detecting those ethical nightmares related to each level of ENC autonomy. (One important resource here would be determining milestones ENC teams may reach such that the organization is comfortable enhancing its autonomy.)

3. Identify what training is needed by those people overseeing the (low/medium/high) autonomous ENC teams.

Perhaps I should have titled this chapter "Fun with Fractals!" I wonder if I can get the cover of the book to represent repeating patterns...

The Ethical Nightmare Challenge for... Everyone

Throughout the last chapter and this one, I have focused on The Ethical Nightmare Challenge as it pertains to ENC teams. And I've been particularly focused on explaining how ENC teams at different levels support each other so that AI project teams can successfully engage in ethical nightmare avoidance, detection, and response. But I have *not* addressed two crucial aspects of AI in organizations.

First, for all AI but especially for generative and agentic AI, a *huge* part of what explains why the AI generates the outputs that it does is the prompt that a user creates for it. I referred to this as SO MANY PROMPTS in Chapter 2. Data scientists and ENC teams can do all sorts of nightmare avoidance, but if the user of the AI is intent on relying on hallucinations, doesn't vet for biased outputs, or is overly deferential to the AI, I'm afraid those end users may well succeed in giving life to a nightmare.

Second, AI is increasingly embedded in everyone's work-flow. *Most* of the contact people have with AI is not playing a role in developing it but in *using* it. More specifically, they are using AI to help them with non-AI specific projects.

When you combine these two facts, you get headlines like, "Deloitte was caught using AI in $290,000 report to help the Australian government crack down on welfare after a researcher flagged hallucinations" with article summaries like, "Deloitte's member firm in Australia will pay the government a partial refund for a $290,000 report that contained alleged AI-generated errors, including references to non-existent academic research papers and a fabricated quote from a federal court judgment."[31] We find similar headlines in other industries: "Trouble with AI 'hallucinations' spreads to big law firms."[32]

What we really get when we combine these two aspects of AI use is that The Ethical Nightmare Challenge doesn't only apply to developing AI. It means that employees and teams that are working on any project in which AI will be used *also* need to take care to avoid AI's ethical nightmares.

This doesn't mean that every project team should engage in the 7-step method. That's too cumbersome and time consuming. Instead, as part of the kickoff of every project the team and/or members of the team should answer the following:

1. What ethical nightmares must be avoided that pertain to our use of AI *in this project*?

2. What are the resources we have to avoid those nightmares?

3. What training, if any, is needed to use those resources?

Suppose the aforementioned Deloitte member firm had gone through this process prior to their work for the Australian government. They could have easily walked out of a 15-minute meeting thinking:

1. We must avoid the ethical nightmare of blindly relying on AI outputs given the known threat of hallucinations *since we'll be using AI to perform basic research throughout this project.*

2. We can fact check ourselves by verifying relevant information without using AI and/or we can run this report by relevant subject matter experts to verify the claims.

3. No special training for this is needed over and above the baseline training we've already received.

Later in the project they could ask themselves whether they executed on (2). If no—get on it! If yes—great! You just avoided a couple hundred thousand dollars in losses and the reputational damage that resulted from dozens of headlines plastered across LinkedIn thousands of times, not to mention your appearance in a certain (bestseller?!) book.

This is the elegant simplicity of The Ethical Nightmare Challenge. It works for developing and deploying AI. It works for executives, department heads, and AI project leaders. It even works for every employee in everyday projects. This is how you create a culture of ethical nightmare avoidance. It's how you create the organizational capacity to build and use AI at scale.

The Grandest of Finales

In Chapters 1 through 3, I noted six seismic shifts from narrow to generative to agentic AI. In case you forgot, here's a summary:

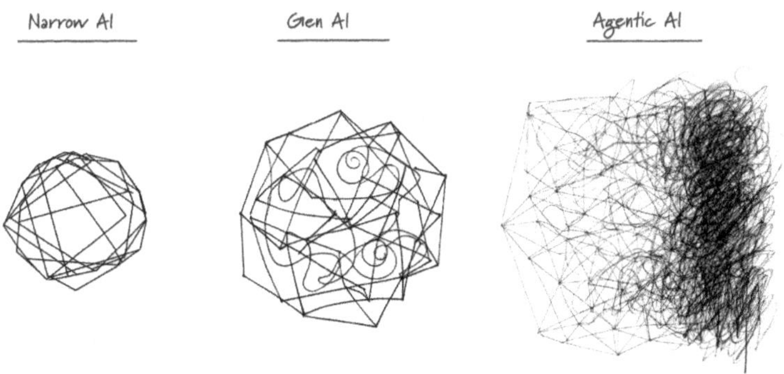

In Chapter 4, I argued that the standard approach to responsible AI can't handle these shifts. Here's a summary of that:

And in Chapters 5 to 7, I presented The Ethical Nightmare Challenge.

The question before us is: how does the ENC manage these seismic shifts? The answer is straightforward.

Each of these seismic shifts can be summarized with a question:

- When in the AI life cycle should risk assessments be performed?

- How do we handle the fact that there is so much unpredictability in how AI acts in the wild?

- Who is responsible when things go sideways?

- Is a human in the loop appropriate?

- What kind of monitoring is needed for this AI?

- How can we communicate and collaborate across the organization to avoid AI ethical nightmares?

The first 5 questions are for ENC teams to answer. They determine when to perform risk assessments, how to monitor AI, who's responsible for what, and so on. The rise of agentic AI entails the need for problem-solving for each AI solution. ENC teams are there to do that problem-solving.

The last question is answered by The Ethical Nightmare Challenge itself. All those people speaking the same language, asking the same questions, and using the same method and tools to answer those questions, *is* organization-wide communication and collaboration.

In closing, here's a summary of that:

And you, too, can rise to The Ethical Nightmare Challenge! Just go to ethicalnightmarechallenge.com. I'll even throw in the T-shirt.

Bring The Ethical Nightmare Challenge to
Your Organization. Learn more:

ACKNOWLEDGMENTS

In my last book, *Ethical Machines*, I acknowledged a range of family and friends for their contributions to my book, my career, and my life more generally. I sang their praises for making my life richer and fuller in more ways than I can count. My grandparents, my parents, and my wife made prominent appearances. It was written with love. It felt like a meaningful thing to do. But I have to acknowledge that I'm much less motivated this time around. I thanked them already – I have to say it again? They didn't get it the first time? It's enough already.

Ethical Machines was a good first book. You think it was very good? Okay, but those are your words, not mine. At any rate, I have to acknowledge that the last few chapters don't stand up tremendously well. They're still relevant – we still need AI ethics committees and the like – but those chapters no longer resemble what we really need, which I hope the ENC captures. I wasn't mistaken when I wrote those chapters, but I must acknowledge that I couldn't see then what I can see now. If you'd like to use chapters 5 and 7 of that book for starting a campfire, I have no objections.

There is, however, one grievous error in *Ethical Machines*. An unforgivable one. I wrote that, were data scientists to invent AGI – artificial general intelligence – then "[i]t could outpunch Rocky, outsmart Sherlock, and out-oppress Pol Pot." But no one, and certainly no damn *thing*, can outpunch

Rocky. I'm ashamed the thought even crossed my mind let alone landed on the page.

I have to acknowledge that while I write on serious topics with serious consequences, I am not a serious man. Clearly. I half-wish I had joined the circus. The other half is regret.

I just got done saying I won't acknowledge friends and family again, but I have to acknowledge I was lying. That's because I must also acknowledge that my wife seemed underwhelmed by my deep expressions of gratitude in my previous book. I don't know why. I said - *and I quote!* - "In all things, if I can move forward, it's only because she has my back." That's not good enough?! It's goddamn poetry! Maybe a little hacky, but certainly a lovely sentiment. There's no satisfying her! But I'll keep trying. For I would do anything for my love, the light of my life, my sun and my moon and my stars and the heavens above, wherein that Goddess deigns to dwell amongst mere mortals. That I should wear shoes before her is an affront. That I should gaze upon her with anything but gratitude is treasonous to love itself. And that she should take me, this wretch, this boy in the garb of a man, this most unworthy one, as her husband, is the apotheosis of Grace.

No? Too much?

ENDNOTES

1   https://www.nytimes.com/2023/07/13/business/media/sag-aftra-writers-strike.html
2   https://www.forbes.com/sites/marisagarcia/2024/02/19/what-air-canada-lost-in-remarkable-lying-ai-chatbot-case/
3   https://www.bbc.com/news/world-us-canada-65735769
4   https://thedailyrecord.com/2025/07/14/ai-use-in-hiring-can-open-legal-issues/
5   https://www.nytimes.com/2026/01/21/business/ai-hiring-tools-lawsuit-eightfold-fcra.html
6   https://fortune.com/2025/10/07/deloitte-ai-australia-government-report-hallucinations-technology-290000-refund/
7   https://fortune.com/2025/11/25/deloitte-caught-fabricated-ai-generated-research-million-dollar-report-canada-government/
8   https://www.washingtonpost.com/style/media/2025/05/20/chicago-sun-times-philadelphia-inquirer-ai-books-summer-reading/
9   https://airisk.mit.edu/ai-incident-tracker#explore-dashboard
10 https://www.wsj.com/tech/ai/anthropic-to-pay-at-least-1-5-billion-in-landmark-copyright-settlement-with-authors-bfcdd57b?gaa_at=eafs&gaa_n=AWEtsqenCrUJPHzqjms_fEZzuUrvkJpwaCq6KHMY-N2wr1JzHug7920zUvph_cX71POc%3D&gaa_ts=6939fa28&gaa_sig=m9DcARQ0uwqcmusb2poh1y3-acJtCc6knxwwNeKoo_x|YyIVZ6AMi4n3iK454wvNjyKLQK7FvUyMJM4XNDK-Wpg%3D%3D
11 https://www.bbc.com/news/articles/cdrkmk00jy0o
12 https://thehackernews.com/2025/11/researchers-find-chatgpt.html?utm_source=chatgpt.com
13 Hicks, Michael Townsen, James Humphries, and Joe Slater. "ChatGPT Is Bullshit." *Ethics and Information Technology* 26, no. 2 (2024): 1–10. *doi:10.1007/s10676-024-09775-5.*
14 https://edition.cnn.com/2023/09/21/us/father-death-google-gps-drive-off-bridge-lawsuit-north-carolina
15 https://www.boston.com/news/local-news/2021/03/15/man-following-gps-navigation-drives-car-into-charlton-lake/

16 https://www.npr.org/2025/07/09/nx-s1-5462609/grok-elon-musk-antisemitic-racist-content

17 https://www.anthropic.com/news/claudes-constitution

18 https://www.anthropic.com/news/claude-new-constitution

19 https://variety.com/2025/digital/news/disney-google-ai-copyright-infringement-cease-and-desist-letter-1236606429/

20 https://www.nature.com/articles/s44387-025-00011-z

21 https://www.bhf.org.uk/informationsupport/heart-matters-magazine/medical/women/misdiagnosis-of-heart-attacks-in-women

22 https://huggingface.co/blog/davidberenstein1957/phare-analysis-of-hallucination-in-leading-llms

23 Still joking!

24 https://www.wired.com/story/truth-terminal-goatse-crypto-millionaire/

25 https://dune.com/seoul/tot

26 Stanley McChrystal et al., *Team of Teams: New Rules of Engagement for a Complex World* (New York: Portfolio/Penguin, 2015), 107.

27 Russo, Richard. *Straight Man*. Vintage Contemporaries, 1997, p. 29.

28 https://www.businessinsider.com/car-dealership-chevrolet-chatbot-chatgpt-pranks-chevy-2023-12

29 https://cset.georgetown.edu/publication/harmonizing-ai-guidance-distilling-voluntary-standards-and-best-practices-into-a-unified-framework/

30 Stanley McChrystal et al., *Team of Teams: New Rules of Engagement for a Complex World* (New York: Portfolio/Penguin, 2015), 153.

31 https://fortune.com/2025/10/07/deloitte-ai-australia-government-report-hallucinations-technology-290000-refund/

32 https://www.reuters.com/legal/government/trouble-with-ai-hallucinations-spreads-big-law-firms-2025-05-23/

Reid Blackman, Ph.D. is the author of *Ethical Machines* (Harvard Business Review Press) and founder and CEO of Virtue Consultants. He has worked with organizations including Amazon, Etsy, Kraft Heinz, Merck, US Bank, and Nationwide to design and implement Responsible AI programs and training. He has also advised the Canadian government on federal AI regulations, served as a founding member of EY's External AI Advisory Board, and was an external Senior Advisor to the Deloitte AI Institute. He is a keynote speaker whose audiences have included the FBI, NASA, and the World Economic Forum. His work has been profiled by The Wall Street Journal, CNN, the BBC, Forbes, and Fox News, and his writing appears in *Harvard Business Review* and *The New York Times*. Prior to founding Virtue, Reid was a professor of philosophy at Colgate University and UNC-Chapel Hill.